PHOTOGRAPHY TEAM
Mike Brunner, Lauren Dorton, Jennifer Dowling, Dustin Weant

PATTERN TEAM
Edie McGinnis, Denise Lane, Jessica Woods, Tyler MacBeth

PROJECT DESIGN TEAM
Jenny Doan, Natalie Earnheart, Janet Yamamoto

EDITOR & COPYWRITERS
Jenny Doan, Natalie Earnheart, Katie Mifsud, Camille Maddox, Nichole Spravzoff, Edie McGinnis

SEWIST TEAM
Jenny Doan, Natalie Earnheart, Janet Yamamoto, Carol Henderson, Denise Lane, Janice Richardson, Jamey Stone

QUILTING & BINDING DEPARTMENT
Betty Bates, Karla Zinkand, Natalie Loucks, Debbie Elder, Jan Meek, Angela Wilson, Chelsea White, Mary McPhee, Charlene McCabe, Dennis Voss, Debbie Allen, Jamee Gilgour, Michelle Templeton, Frank Jones, Kara Snow, Ethan Lucas, Devin Ragle, Bruce VanIperen, Lyndia Lovell, Aaron Crawford, Cyera Cottrill, Deborah Warner, Salena Smiley, Francesca Flemming, Rachael Joyce, Bernice Kelly, Deloris Burnett

LOCATION CREDIT
Morrell Ranch
21708 Nickle Ave
Gallatin, MO 64640

PRINTING COORDINATORS
Rob Stoebener, Seann Dwyer

PRINTING SERVICES
Walsworth Print Group
803 South Missouri
Marceline, MO 64658

CONTACT US
Missouri Star Quilt Company
114 N Davis
Hamilton, MO 64644
888-571-1122
info@missouriquiltco.com

content

Oops! Sometimes we make mistakes.
To find corrections to every issue of Block
go to: **www.msqc.co/corrections**

hello
from MSQC

Summer is almost here and I can't wait! I recently took a trip to the beautiful Pacific Northwest and everywhere I looked trees were in bloom, flowers were opening, and greenery seemed to fill every crack in the sidewalk. There wasn't a bare spot of earth without new growth!

Looking down at those mossy cracks in the sidewalk reminded me that no matter where I am in life, there's always room for growth. Even if it seems like there's hardly any space for something new, there's always room for improvement. Now, don't get me wrong, I like to keep things simple. I don't think improvement necessarily means adding a new checklist to my daily routine, but it means being more mindful about what I am actually doing.

That's why I truly believe that the little things matter. Smiling at the cashier at the grocery store matters. Taking the time to stitch up a gift for a friend matters. Sending a short "Thank You" card can mean the world to someone who reached out to you. All of these little things add up to one big thing in life: gratitude. I believe gratitude can take us from misery to happiness. Thank you for being who you are and spreading joy with all the little things you do.

JENNY DOAN
MISSOURI STAR QUILT CO

TRY OUR APP

It's easy to keep up on every issue of BLOCK magazine. Access it from all your devices. And when you subscribe to BLOCK, it's free with your subscription! For the app search BLOCK magazine in the app store. Available for both Apple and Android.

totally tulips

A celery seed is tiny—no bigger than the period at the end of this sentence. But each little seed holds plenty of potential. Just one ounce can produce an entire acre of fully grown celery plants. Why do I know this? Because, believe it or not, I used to work on a celery farm. It's true!

For many years, Missouri has been my home, but I actually grew up in an agricultural region of central California known as the Salinas Valley. The temperate coastal climate and rich soil of that area produce so many fruits and vegetables, it is sometimes called "The Salad Bowl of the World." It's a beautiful place, where neatly planted rows of broccoli, lettuce, and strawberries stretch over gently rolling hills like an enormous patchwork quilt.

Almost 95% of the celery produced in the United States is grown right in those fields, so when it came time to get my very first summer job, there was plenty of opportunity to work. My school choir was planning a trip and I was determined to save enough money to go, so into the fields I went.

Young celery grown from seed has to be pulled up, separated, and replanted in order to give each plant the space it needs. Dressed in my old jeans and work boots, I knelt in the dirt to pull out the little baby celery plants. Each tiny plant, one by one, had to be carefully picked and separated by hand. It was hard, dirty work, but I stuck with it and earned the cash I needed. Years

For the tutorial and everything you need to make this quilt visit www.msqc.co/blocksummer18

later, I can't pass a display of celery stalks in the grocery store without thinking of all the work that went into those simple green veggies.

Each of us has our own "first job" story. During high school, one friend spent her summers washing dishes at a Scout camp on Catalina Island. The pay wasn't great, and the work wasn't glamorous, but she sure had fun! She developed wonderful friendships with fellow staff members, and every day after the last dish was scrubbed, she headed to the beach to snorkel with vividly orange Garibaldi fish the size of dinner plates.

Another friend worked all summer long repainting classrooms, scrubbing graffiti off bathroom stalls, and scraping gum from the bottom of desks. Boy oh boy, did she learn a lesson about respecting public property!

And one of our own Missouri Star employees spent her teenage summers volunteering as a candy striper at the local hospital. The hours she spent serving those patients cultivated compassion and left her with a lifetime of sweet memories.

A first job experience leaves such an impression on your mind. Whether it's burger flipping or sweeping up popcorn at the movie theater, a young person learns so much about hard work and responsibility. A summer job may only last a few months, but those lessons last a lifetime!

materials

QUILT SIZE
89" X 90"

BLOCK SIZE
9" x 17" finished

QUILT TOP
1 package 10" print squares
¼ yard solid
3½ yards background fabric –
  includes inner border

OUTER BORDER
1½ yards

BINDING
¾ yard

BACKING
2¾ yards - 108" wide

SAMPLE QUILT
Butterfly Dance by Sally Kelly for
Windham fabrics

1 cut

Select (28) 10" print squares. Cut each in half vertically and horizontally to make 5" squares for a **total of 112.** The remaining squares will be used for "leaves."

From the ¼ yard of solid fabric, cut:
• (28) 1½" x 8½" rectangles. Cut the pieces vertically to make the most of your fabric.

From the background fabric, cut:
• (4) 10" strips across the width of the fabric. Subcut the strips into 10" squares. Each strip will yield 4 squares and you need 14. Set the extra squares aside for another project.

• (14) 2½" strips across the width of the fabric. Subcut 7 strips into 2½" squares. Each strip will yield 16 squares and a **total of 112** squares are needed. Subcut the remaining 7 strips into 2½" x 9½" rectangles. Each strip will yield 4 rectangles and a **total of 28** are needed. Set these pieces aside to use for sashing rectangles.

Set the remaining fabric aside for the long sashing strips and the inner border.

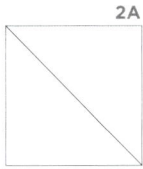

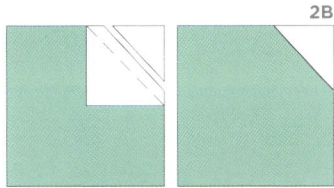

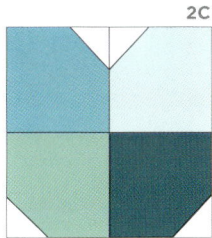

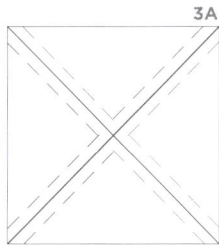

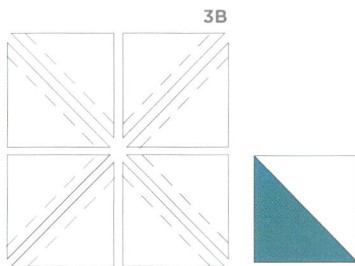

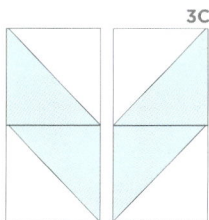

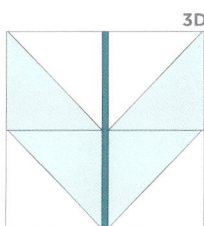

2 mark and sew

On the reverse side of the 2½" squares, mark a line from corner to corner once on the diagonal either by folding the square and pressing in a crease or by marking it with a pencil. **2A**

Place a marked background square atop a 5" print square with right sides facing. Sew on the marked line. Trim the excess fabric away ¼" from the sewn seam. **Make 112. 2B**

Sew 4 snowballed squares together in 2 rows of 2. The first row has the snowballed squares meeting in the center. The second row has the snowballed squares turned away from the center. Sew the 2 rows together. **Make 28** and set aside for the moment. These units will be used as the tulip blossoms. **2C**

3 leaf units

On the reverse side of 14 background 10" squares, draw a line from corner to corner twice on the diagonal. Layer a marked 10" square with a print 10" square with right side facing. Sew on either side of both drawn lines using a ¼" seam allowance. **3A**

Cut the sewn squares through the center horizontally and vertically. Then cut on the drawn lines. Open each section to reveal a half-square triangle. Each set of sewn squares yield 8 half-square triangles and you need a **total of 112.**

Square each half-square triangle unit to 4½" and stack the matching half-square triangles together. **3B**

Pick up 4 matching half-square triangles. Sew 2 together in a vertical row as shown. Notice the direction in which the half-square triangles are placed. Sew the other 2 matching half-square triangles together in the same manner. Notice the half-square triangles are placed in the opposite direction of the first row, creating a mirror image. **3C**

Sew the vertical rows to either side of a solid 1½" x 8½" rectangle. **Make 28 leaf units. 3D**

4 join units

Sew a blossom unit to a leaf unit as shown to complete the block. **Make 28 blocks. 4A**

Sew a 2½" x 9½" background rectangle to the bottom of 14 blocks. Sew a 2½" x 9½" background rectangle to the top of the remaining blocks. **4B**

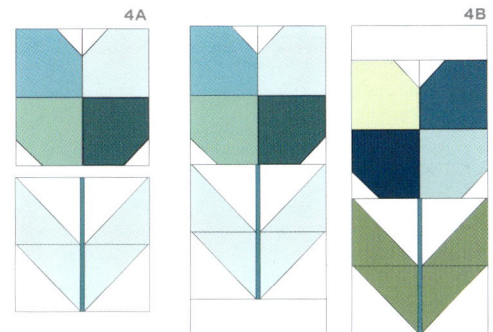

1 Place a marked background square atop a 5″ print square with right sides facing. Sew on the marked line, then trim ¼″ away from the sewn seam.

2 Press the seam allowance of the snowballed square toward the print fabric. Make 4.

3 Sew 4 snowballed 5″ squares together in a 4-patch formation as shown.

4 Make leaf units by stitching 2 half-square triangles together vertically. Notice the 2 leaf units are mirror images of each other. Sew a leaf unit to either side of a 1½″ x 8½″ solid rectangle.

5 Sew a tulip top to a tulip stem unit to complete the block.

6 Add a 2½″ x 9½″ background rectangle to the bottom of 14 tulip blocks. Sew a 2½″ x 9½″ rectangle to the top of the remaining blocks.

5 putting it all together

Lay out the blocks in **vertical** rows with each row having 4 blocks. Begin the first row with blocks that have the background rectangle sewn to the bottom of the block. Alternate that row with blocks that have the background rectangle sewn to the top of the block. Continue on in this manner until you have 7 rows. Sew the rows together vertically when you are happy with the arrangement.

6 make vertical sashing strips

From the remaining background fabric, cut:

- (12) 2½" strips across the width of the fabric. Remove the selvages and sew 2 strips together end-to-end. Measure the row of blocks and trim the strip to your measurement. It should be approximately 76½". **Make 6.**

Join the rows, adding a sashing strip between each to complete the center of the quilt top.

7 inner border

Cut (8) 2½" strips across the width of the fabric. Sew the strips together end-to-end to make one long strip. Trim the borders from this strip.

Refer to Borders (pg. 102) in the Construction Basics to measure and cut the inner borders. The strips are approximately 76½" for the sides and approximately 79½" for the top and bottom.

8 outer border

Cut (9) 5½" strips across the width of the fabric. Sew the strips together end-to-end to make one long strip. Trim the borders from this strip.

Refer to Borders (pg. 102) in the Construction Basics to measure and cut the outer borders. The strips are approximately 80½" for the sides and approximately 89½" for the top and bottom.

9 quilt and bind

Layer the quilt with batting and backing and quilt. After the quilting is complete, square up the quilt and trim away all excess batting and backing. Add binding to complete the quilt. See Construction Basics (pg. 102) for binding instructions.

For the tutorial and everything
you need to make this quilt visit:
www.msqc.co/blocksummer18

spring
rain

Camping in Missouri is pure bliss. We have beautiful state parks where we go every summer as a family to relax, ride motorcycles, and sing around the campfire. There's nothing like a Doan family camping trip on a warm night. The crackle of the fire and the hum of sweet voices has got to be one of my favorite sounds in the entire world.

Sitting around the campfire always feels like a special time with the family. Each night we gather together after our day's adventures and tell stories, sing songs, and toast marshmallows, along with other goodies. Sometimes we go around the circle and tell our favorite part of the day or what we like about each other, which is a wonderful way to feel closer. But one thing that's for certain, there's always plenty of good food to go around after a full day out in the woods.

I tend to think that an event is only about as good as the food, so camping must also include delicious treats! For some reason, cooking around a campfire makes everything taste absolutely amazing. Maybe it's because we've all worked up healthy appetites, but maybe it's something more. We haul out our heavy, cast iron dutch ovens on each trip and boy, is it worth it.

If you've never cooked in a dutch oven, this is something you've got to try! I dare you to put the most ordinary ingredients inside and see what they can become! A can of simple beef stew with prepackaged biscuits on top becomes a meal to remember. A store bought box of cake mix with pineapple and brown sugar on the bottom turns into the best pineapple upside down cake of your life! It's pure magic.

DUTCH OVEN
PINEAPPLE
Upside Down Cake

12" cast iron Dutch oven	1 cup brown sugar
Aluminum foil	1 small jar maraschino
24 charcoal briquettes	cherries
1 8 oz. can of pineapple	1 box yellow cake mix
slices in juice	3 eggs
½ cup butter	⅓ cup vegetable oil

Prepare the Dutch oven by lining it with aluminum foil and lighting about 24 charcoal briquettes. They are ready when they turn white hot. Drain the pineapple slices, reserving the juice. Melt butter in the bottom of the foil-lined Dutch oven, then evenly sprinkle the brown sugar over the butter. Arrange the pineapple slices on the brown sugar mixture in a single layer and place cherries in each hole of the pineapple rings. Combine cake mix, eggs, oil, and pineapple juice, according to cake mix directions, replacing the water with the pineapple juice. Gently pour the cake batter over the pineapple. Replace the lid, then put 12 coals on the lid and 12 underneath the Dutch oven. Bake for about 30 minutes until the top of cake is golden brown and a toothpick comes out clean. Enjoy!

materials

QUILT SIZE
82" x 94"

BLOCK SIZE
10" finished

QUILT TOP
1 package 10" squares
3 yards background fabric
1¼ yards contrasting print

OUTER BORDER
1½ yards

BINDING
¾ yard

BACKING
7½ yards - horizontal seam(s)
or 2½ yards 108" wide

SAMPLE QUILT
Chantrell by Anne Rowan for
Wilmington Prints

1 make half-square triangles

Draw a line from corner to corner twice on the diagonal on the reverse side of a light 10" square. Layer the square with a darker print with right sides facing. Sew ¼" away from each side of the drawn lines. Cut through the center horizontally and vertically. Then cut on the drawn lines. Each set of sewn squares will yield 8 half-square triangle units. **1A**

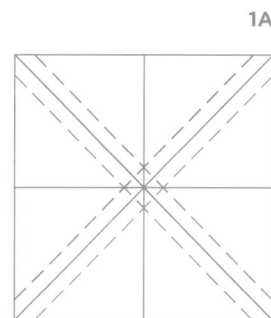

1A

1B

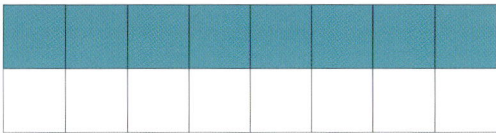
3A

2½"

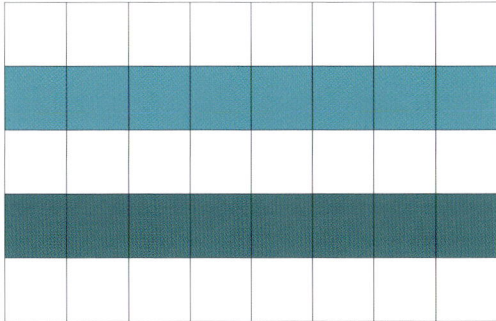
3B

2½"

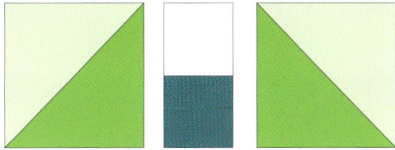
4A

4B

Open the half-square triangle units and press the seam allowance toward the darker fabric. Square up each half-square triangle to 4½". **1B Make 168**

2 cut

From the background fabric, cut:
- (40) 2½" strips across the width of the fabric.

From the contrasting print fabric, cut:
- (16) 2½" strips across the width of the fabric.

3 make strip sets

Sew a background 2½" strip to a contrasting print 2½" strip. Make 6 sets and cut each of them into 2½" increments for a **total of 84**. **3A**

Sew 3 background strips and 2 contrasting print strips together to make a strip set. Alternate the background strips with the print strips. Make 3 strip sets like this and cut each of the sets into 2½" increments for a **total of 42**. **3B**

4 block construction

Sew a half-square triangle unit to either side of a small strip set. Make 2 rows like this for each block. **4A**

Sew a half-square triangle row to either side of a large strip set to complete the block. **4B**

Block size: 10" finished
Make 42

5 arrange blocks

Arrange the blocks to your satisfaction into 7 rows with each row having 6 blocks.

6 cut

From the remaining 2½" background strips, cut:
- (97) 2½" x 10½" rectangles

From the remaining 2½" contrasting strips, cut:
- (56) 2½" squares

7 sew

Sew a 2½" x 10½" sashing rectangle between each block vertically. Add a sashing rectangle to both ends of each row as well. You should have 7 sashed rows. **7A**

Make a horizontal sashing strip by sewing cornerstones and sashing rectangles together. Begin with a cornerstone and add a sashing rectangle. Continue on in this manner until you have sewn a row that has 7 cornerstones and 6 sashing rectangles. **7B Make 8**

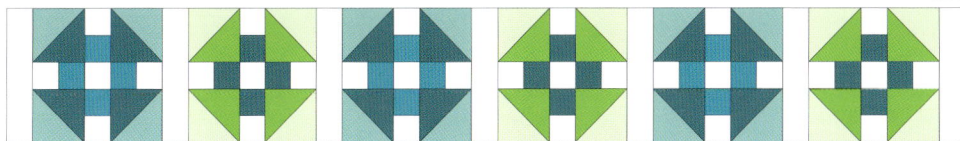
7A

7B

1   Draw a line from corner to corner twice on the diagonal on the reverse side of a light 10″ square. Layer the marked square with a darker print with right sides facing. Sew on either side of all the lines using a ¼″ seam allowance. Cut in half vertically and horizontally, then cut on the drawn lines.

2   Open the half-square triangle units and press the seam allowance toward the darker fabric. Square each to 4½″.

3   Make a small strip set by sewing a dark 2½″ strip to a light 2½″ strip. Cut into 2½″ increments.

4   Make a large strip set by sewing 3 background strips and 2 print strips together. Alternate the 2 colors. Cut into 2½″ increments.

5   To make the top and bottom rows of the block, sew a half-square triangle unit to either side of a small strip set.

6   Sew the top and bottom row to either side of a large strip set increment to complete the block.

Sew the rows together, adding a horizontal sashing strip between each. Add a sashing strip to the top and bottom of the rows, as well.

8 border

Cut (9) 4½" strips across the width of the fabric. Sew the strips together end-to-end to make one long strip. Trim the borders from this strip.

Refer to Borders (pg. 102) in the Construction Basics to measure and cut the borders. The strips are approximately 86½" for the sides and approximately 82½" for the top and bottom.

9 quilt and bind

Layer the quilt with batting and backing and quilt. After the quilting is complete, square up the quilt and trim away all excess batting and backing. Add binding to complete the quilt. See Construction Basics (pg. 102) for binding instructions.

easy breezy
beautiful

In the heat of the summer, afternoons are usually slow and lazy. The air is so heavy and hot, everyone seems to retreat inside to wait for the cooler temperatures after sunset. Kids that spent the morning riding bikes and running through sprinklers are now nearly comatose in front of the television. But there is one sound that can bring those hot, sweaty kids back to life in an instant: the ice cream truck.

That familiar music box rendition of "The Entertainer" floats across the sticky afternoon air, and the entire atmosphere transforms. Kids are up and out the door, pricking up their ears to discern the location of the truck. Is it down the street? Is it around the block? Is it headed the other way? An opportunity like this can't be missed, so with crinkled dollar bills held tight in clenched fists, they hop on their bikes to chase down that truck.

When I was little, I always ordered a cherry-pineapple flavored popsicle called "The Big Stick." It was so sweet and cold, and it lasted much longer than a regular twin pop. Best of all, those bright red and yellow swirls turned my lips a fiery shade of red. I can remember staring in the mirror with puckered lips to admire my beautiful "lipstick."

For the tutorial and everything you need to make this quilt visit:
www.msqc.co/blocksummer18

Of course, if you don't have an ice cream truck in your town, you can always make your own frozen treats. Jennie Wiedmaier here at Missouri Star has fond memories of making homemade ice cream as a child.

Jennie's grandmother had a hand-cranked ice cream maker, and Jennie and her sister took turns cranking the handle until the ice cream was thick and creamy. They almost always made banana flavored ice cream, but at the end of the summer when the peaches started to ripen, peach ice cream became a favorite.

Jennie also remembers making ice cream in coffee cans at vacation bible school. Whole milk, cream, and sugar were mixed in a one-pound coffee can. After making sure the lid was on tight, the can was placed inside of a larger coffee can, and ice and rock salt were poured on top. The children sat on the floor and rolled the can between them until the ice cream was ready to eat.

At the end of a hot summer day, there just isn't anything like sitting down with friends and family for a nice, cool treat. Thank goodness for ice cream!

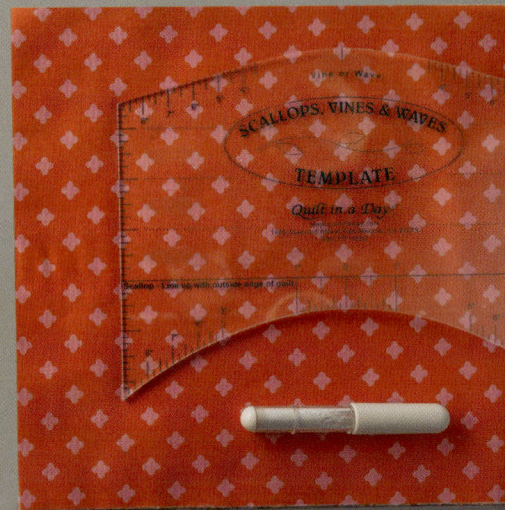

materials

QUILT SIZE
76" x 85½"

BLOCK SIZE
9½" finished

QUILT TOP
1 package 10" print squares

INNER BORDER
¾ yard

OUTER BORDER
2 yards

BINDING
1 yard

BACKING
7¼ yards - horizontal seam(s)

OTHER
Scallops, Vines & Waves Template
  by Quilt in a Day
Clover Pen Style Chaco Liner White

SAMPLE QUILT
Club Havana by Patty Young for
Riley Blake Designs

1 sew

Arrange the 10" print squares into rows. Each row is made up of 6 squares across and 7 rows are needed. Sew the squares into rows. Press the seam allowances of the even rows toward the right and the odd rows toward the left to make the seams "nest." Join the rows to complete the center of the quilt.

2 inner border

Cut (7) 2½" strips across the width of the fabric. Sew the strips together end-to-end to make one long strip. Trim the borders from this strip.

Refer to Borders (pg. 102) in the Construction Basics to measure and cut the inner borders. The strips are approximately 67" for the sides and approximately 61½" for the top and bottom.

3 outer border

Cut (8) 8" strips across the width of the fabric. Sew the strips together end-

completed, use the Scallops, Vines and Waves template to mark the scallops just inside the outer edge of the quilt. (Follow the instructions included in the booklet that comes with the template for measuring directions.) Cut the scalloped edge.

5 make bias binding

Because the edges have been scalloped, you will need to make bias binding. From the binding fabric, cut a 34" square. Fold the square from corner to corner once on the diagonal (a 45° angle). Press a crease in place along the diagonal fold. Place a ruler on the crease, and cut 2½" strips. You'll need enough strips to measure at least 350" after the strips have been sewn together. Refer to page 102 in the Construction Basics and use the Plus Sign method to join the strips.

After the strips have been joined, gently press the strip in half with wrong sides together. Sew the binding to the front of the quilt, then fold to the back and whipstitch in place.

to-end to make one long strip. Trim the borders from this strip.

Refer to Borders (pg. 102) in the Construction Basics to measure and cut the outer borders. The strips are approximately 71" for the sides and approximately 76½" for the top and bottom.

4 quilt and bind

Layer the quilt with batting and backing and quilt. After the quilting has been

1 Use the Scallops, Vines and Waves template by Quilt in a Day to mark the scallops just inside the outer edge of the quilt. Follow the instructions included in the booklet that comes with the template.

2 Using scissors, begin cutting the scalloped edge at one corner.

3 Continue cutting until all the scallops have been cut.

4 Begin applying bias binding on one edge of a scallop. Be sure to leave at least a 10″ tail free so it will be easy to connect the binding when you get back to the start.

5 When you reach the peak of a scallop, stop sewing, lift the presser foot and pivot the binding and the edge of the quilt, then continue sewing the binding in place.

6 After the binding has been applied to the front of the quilt, flip it over and whipstitch the binding to the back.

28

HSTs
around
the world

June nights in Missouri are magical. The sun sets, the sky starts to darken, and hundreds—maybe thousands—of lightning bugs come out to play. They glow and flash like fairy lights dancing in the shadows of trees and bushes.

Like so many other creatures, a firefly's showiness is all for the sake of romance. Male fireflies hover through the air flashing amorous messages to the lady fireflies relaxing on the grass below. If a female is impressed, she blinks a response with her own little light.

One of our gals here at Missouri Star, remembers spending summers at her grandparents' farm. "At dusk the fireflies began to flicker and shine. It reminded me of the twinkling of the stars above."

For the tutorial and everything you need to make this quilt visit: **www.msqc.co/blocksummer18**

She continues, "When my boys were young, they loved to catch fireflies in jars to make lanterns. If one got squished, the boys were happy to smear the goop on their arms to make glow streaks. Year after year, those fireflies brought an extra bit of magic to our summer nights."

Edie Mcginnis, another member of the Missouri Star team, shared her childhood memories of fireflies in the summer. Her words, I think, perfectly describe the experience of so many Midwestern children.

"Lightning bugs appeared at twilight. There we were, three little girls holding a mason jar at the ready. All we needed was one glimmer of light, one spark and we were off. Chasing, running, sneaking quietly, we each had our own method while we were on the hunt. When we had enough bugs in our jars, we added a little grass that was wet with dew so the bugs could get a drink. Then we slipped back into the house in search of a lid. My oldest sister poked holes in the lids with a butcher knife so our bugs would be able to breathe. After going to bed, we lay there and watched our jars of bugs lighting up our bedroom as we drifted off to sleep."

I've traveled the world and seen the twinkling lights of many beautiful cities, but nothing quite compares to the magic of a firefly show in my very own backyard.

materials

QUILT SIZE
57" X 69"

BLOCK SIZE
6" finished

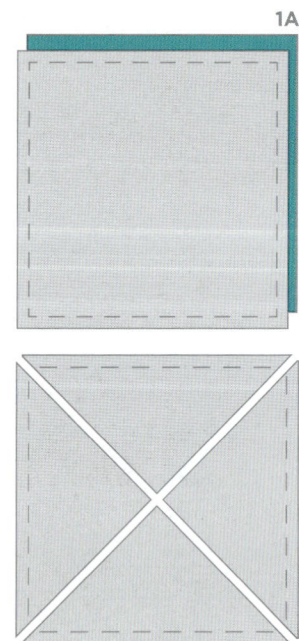

QUILT TOP
1 packages 10" squares

BORDER
1 yard

BINDING
¾ yard

BACKING
3¾ yards - horizontal seam(s)

SAMPLE QUILT
Blossom Batiks Splash by Flaurie & Finch for RJR Fabrics

1 cut and sew

Separate the 10" squares into 2 stacks, one of light fabrics and the other of darks (20 of each). Pair a light square with a dark square. Sew all the way around the outer edge using a ¼" seam allowance. Cut the sewn square from corner to corner twice on the diagonal to make 4 half-square triangle units. Open, press and trim each to 6½".

Make 80. 1A

Block Size: 6" Finished

1A

2 arrange the blocks

Follow the diagram to the left and arrange the blocks. Be aware of how you are placing the light and dark part of the half-square triangles. Sew the half-square triangles into **rows of 8**. You'll need to make **10 rows**. 1B

Sew the rows together.

3 border

Cut (6) 5" strips across the width of the fabric. Sew the strips together end-to-end to make one long strip. Trim the borders from this strip.

Refer to Borders (pg. 102) in the Construction Basics to measure and cut the inner borders. The strips are approximately 60½" for the sides and approximately 57½" for the top and bottom.

4 quilt and bind

Layer the quilt with batting and backing and quilt. After the quilting is complete, square up the quilt and trim away all excess batting and backing. Add binding to complete the quilt. See Construction Basics (pg. 102) for binding instructions.

1 Pair a light 10″ square with a dark 10″ square. Sew all the way around the outer perimeter using a ¼″ seam allowance.

2 Cut the sewn squares from corner to corner twice on the diagonal.

3 Open each section to reveal a half-square triangle unit. Square each to 6½″.

bonus project

bordering triangle table runner

materials

TABLE RUNNER SIZE
23" X 39"

BLOCK SIZE
4" finished

TABLE RUNNER TOP
1 package 5" squares

INNER BORDER
¼ yard

OUTER BORDER
½ yard

BINDING
½ yard

BACKING
1½ yards - horizontal seam(s)

SAMPLE TABLE RUNNER
Blossom Batiks Splash by Flaurie & Finch for RJR Fabrics

1A

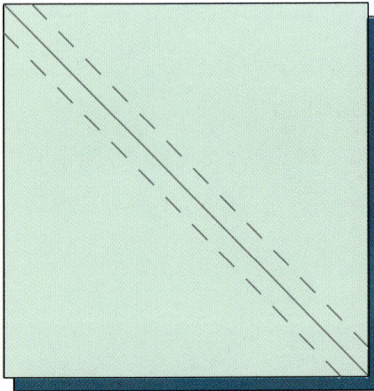

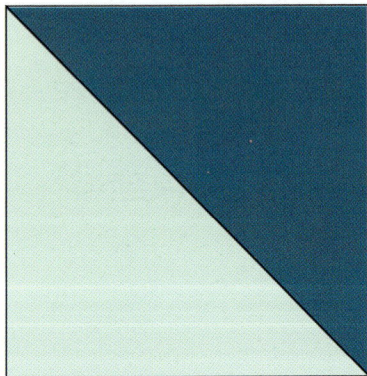

1 sew

Draw a line from corner to corner once on the diagonal on the reverse side of 16 light print 5″ squares. Layer a marked light 5″ print square with a dark 5″ square with right sides facing. Sew on both sides of the drawn line using a ¼″ seam allowance. Cut on the drawn line. Open to reveal 2 half-square triangles. Press the seam toward the darker fabric. Square each half-square triangle to 4½″.

Make a total of 32. 1A

Block Size: 4″ finished

2 arrange and sew

Arrange the blocks into rows. Each row is made up of 4 blocks and 8 rows are needed. Refer to the diagram on page 39 for color placement of each half-square triangle block. When you are satisfied with the arrangement, sew the blocks into rows. Press the seams of the odd rows toward the right and the even rows toward the left to make the seams "nest." Join the rows together.

3 inner border

Cut (3) 1½″ strips across the width of the fabric. Sew the strips together end-to-end to make one long strip. Trim the borders from this strip.

Refer to Borders (pg. 102) in the Construction Basics to measure and cut the inner borders. The strips are approximately 16½″ for the short ends and approximately 34½″ for the top and bottom.

4 outer border

Cut (3) 3″ strips across the width of the fabric. Sew the strips together end-to-end to make one long strip. Trim the borders from this strip.

Refer to Borders (pg. 102) in the Construction Basics to measure and cut the outer borders. The strips are approximately 18½″ for the short ends and approximately 39½″ for the top and bottom.

5 quilt and bind

Layer the table runner with batting and backing and quilt. After the quilting is complete, square up the table runner and trim away all excess batting and backing. Add binding to complete the table runner. See Construction Basics (pg. 102) for binding instructions.

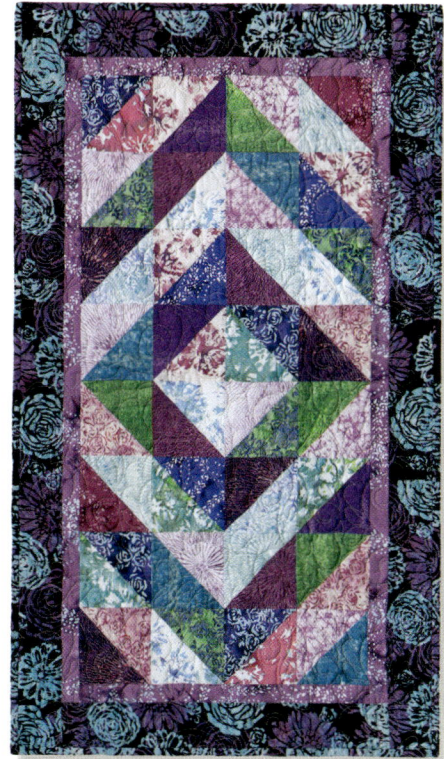

sidekick

A drive with the Doans is never quiet. We are car singers! Our kids grew up before handheld devices, so to entertain each other in the car, we sang . . . a lot! Show tunes, oldies, camp songs, the louder the better! One year I made a rule that every time we saw an American flag, we had to sing "You're a Grand Old Flag." Well, that was fine until the Fourth of July when there were flags everywhere! We couldn't get through the first verse before we passed a another flag and had to start over.

Here in the country, you can drive for miles past beautiful green pastures and golden wheatfields. You may pass a cow or two—maybe a fancy barn if you're lucky—but it really is "the open road."

On warm summer evenings, it's so fun to hop in the car, make a quick stop at a drive-through for a soft serve twist cone, and head out for a little joyride. It doesn't really matter where you're headed; with the radio on and the windows down, an hour or two on the road can feel like its own little adventure.

A few years ago, my friends Allison and Isaac decided to take their kids for an afternoon drive through the canyon near their Rocky Mountain home. They invited another family to come along, and both minivans were packed with

For the tutorial and everything
you need to make this quilt visit:
www.msqc.co/blocksummer18

picnic blankets, sandwiches, juice boxes, and a total of four parents and eight children.

They started up the mountains, eventually taking an unpaved side road that led to a nice picnic spot next to a quiet stream. The wheels rolled slowly over small rocks and uneven ground when suddenly, POP! Allison and Isaac's rear passenger tire blew. After a quick tire change, they were once again on their way. But just as they arrived at their picnic destination, POP! Another tire gave up the ghost. Isaac hopped out to survey the situation only to discover that the spare tire was also losing air. What are the chances? Three flat tires in under five minutes!

So, while Isaac and his friend drove the functioning vehicle back to town to buy tires, the women and children had a ball picnicking, exploring, and throwing rocks into a nearby stream. They counted twenty-five different varieties of wildflowers and watched chipmunks scurry along fallen tree trunks.

A few hours—and several hundred dollars—later, they were back on the road headed home. It was almost dark outside, and Isaac was feeling tired and a bit discouraged. Suddenly, five-year-old Emma called from the back seat of the van, "Dad, that was so fun! Can we go on a drive again?" And so they did. Every single Saturday for the rest of the summer, that little family drove to destinations near and far, and those expensive new tires kept them safe and rolling all along the way.

materials

QUILT SIZE
59" x 71"

BLOCK SIZE
12" finished

QUILT TOP
3 packages 5" print squares
2 packages 5" background squares

INNER BORDER
½ yard

OUTER BORDER
1 yard

BINDING
¾ yard

BACKING
3¾ yards - horizontal seam(s)

SAMPLE QUILT
High Adventure 2 by Design by Dani
for Riley Blake Designs

1 block construction

Select 2 matching 5" print squares. Trim 1 to 4½" and cut the other 1 into (4) 2½" squares. Keep all matching prints together. Set aside for the moment.

Select 2 different pairs of matching print 5" squares. Draw a line from corner to corner once on the diagonal on the reverse side of (4) 5" background squares. Layer a marked background 5" square with a 5" print square. Sew on both sides of the drawn line using a ¼" seam allowance. Cut on the drawn line to reveal 2 half-square triangles. Open each and press the seam allowance toward

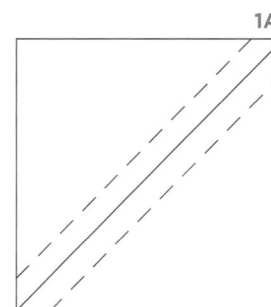

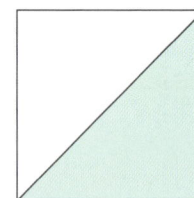

1A

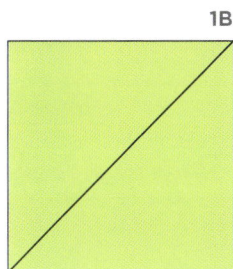
1B

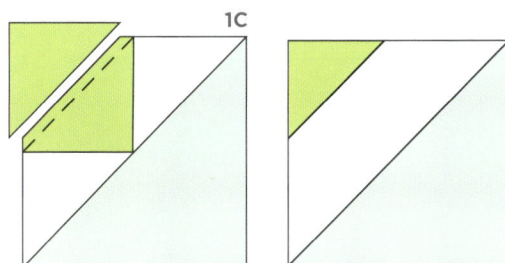
1C

1D

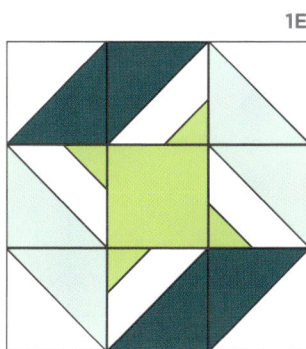
1E

the darker fabric. You should have a total of 8 half-square triangles that include 4 matching one print and 4 matching the other. Square each half-square triangle to 4½". **1A**

Pick up the (4) 2½" squares that match the center 4½" print square. Draw a line from corner to corner once on the diagonal on the reverse side of each of the squares. **1B**

Place a marked print square on the background corner of 2 matching half-square triangles and on the background corner of 2 of the other matching half-square triangles. Sew on the drawn line to snowball each of the 4 half-square triangles. Trim the excess fabric ¼" away from the sewn seam. Press the seam allowance toward the darker fabric. **1C**

Lay out the units that make up the block into a 9-patch formation as shown. Notice that the snowballed corners of the half-square triangles touch the center square. **1D**

Sew the units into rows, then sew the rows together to complete the block. Make 20 blocks. **1E**

Block Size: 12" finished

2 arrange and sew

Arrange the blocks into rows. Each row is made up of 4 blocks and 5 rows are needed. When you are satisfied with the arrangement, sew the blocks into rows. Press the seams of the odd rows toward the right and the even rows toward the left. Then sew the rows together.

3 inner border

Cut (6) 2½" strips across the width of the fabric. Sew the strips together end-to-end to make one long strip. Trim the borders from this strip.

Refer to Borders (pg. 102) in the Construction Basics to measure and cut the inner borders. The strips are approximately 60½" for the sides and approximately 52½" for the top and bottom.

4 outer border

Cut (7) 4" strips across the width of the fabric. Sew the strips together end-to-end to make one long strip. Trim the borders from this strip.

Refer to Borders (pg. 102) in the Construction Basics to measure and cut the outer borders. The strips are

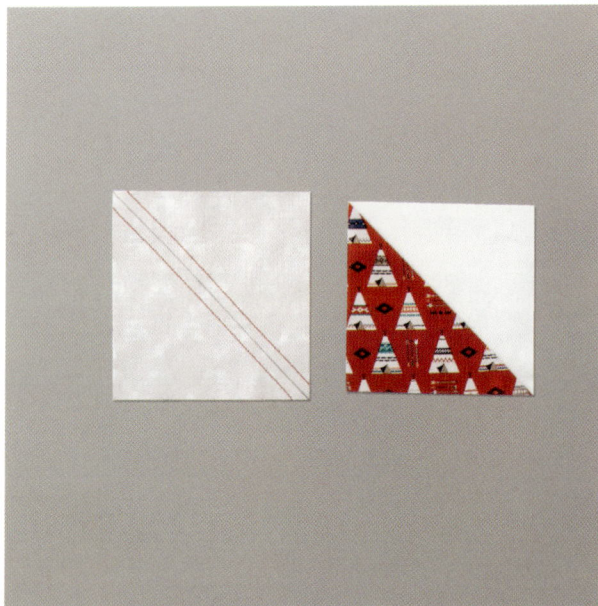

1 Draw a line from corner to corner once on the diagonal on the reverse side of a background square. Layer with a 5″ print square with right sides facing and sew on both sides of the line using a ¼″ seam allowance. Cut on the drawn line and open to reveal 2 half-square triangle units.

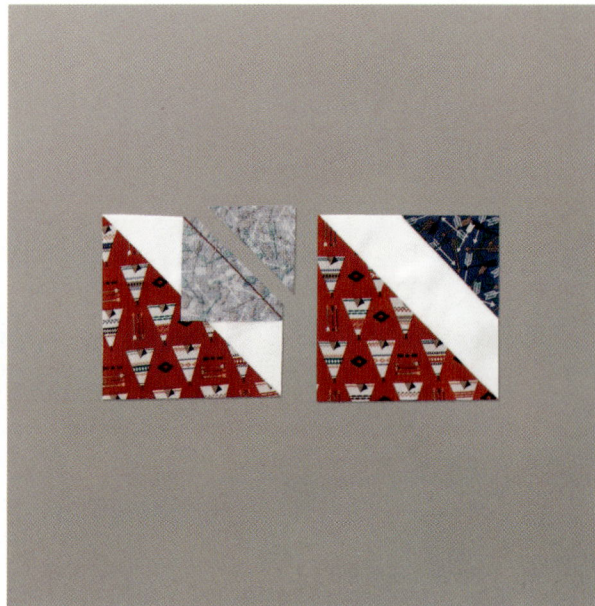

2 Place a marked print square on the background corner of 2 matching half-square triangles and sew on the drawn line. Trim the excess fabric away ¼″ from the sewn seam.

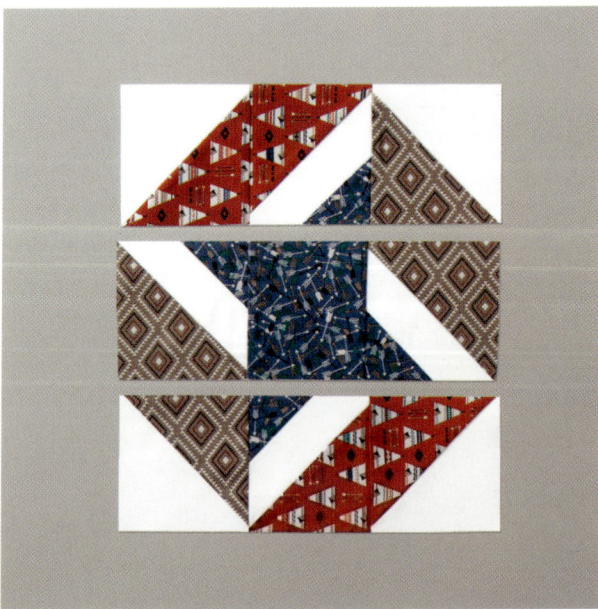

3 Lay out the units that make up the block into a 9-patch formation as shown. Sew the units into rows.

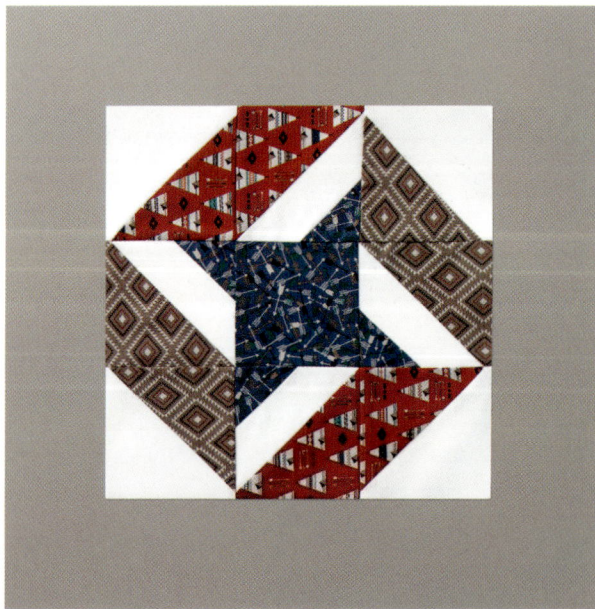

4 Sew the rows together to complete the block.

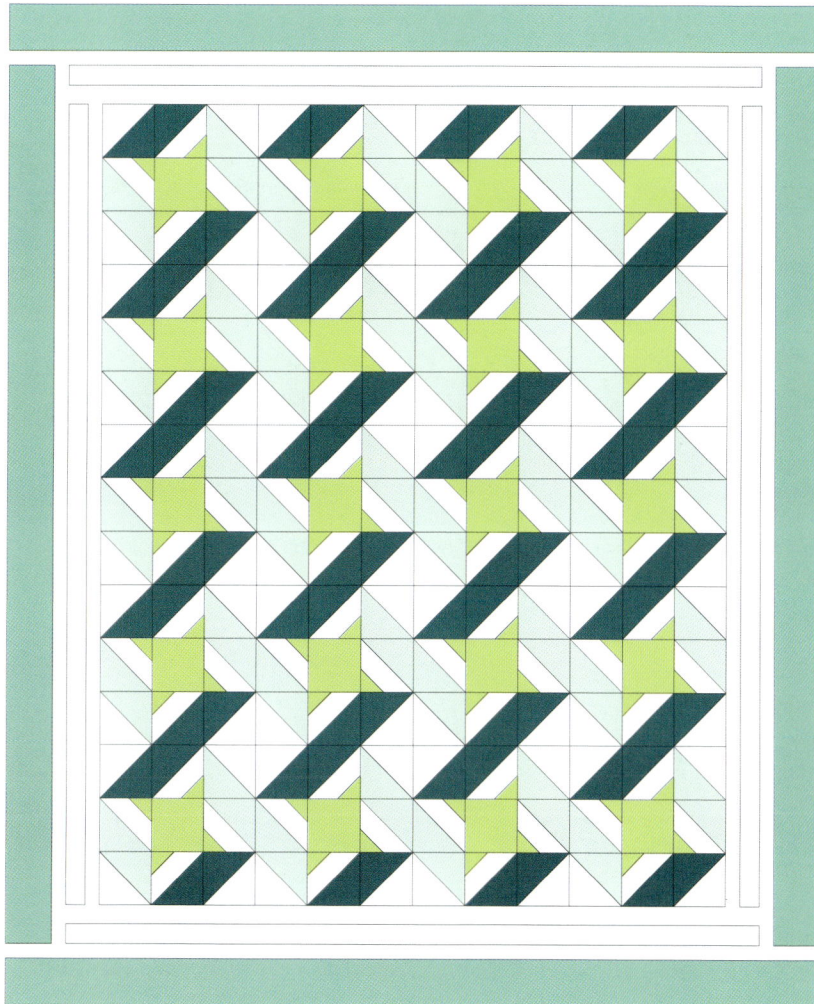

approximately 64½″ for the sides and approximately 59½″ for the top and bottom.

5 quilt and bind

Layer the quilt with batting and backing and quilt. After the quilting is complete, square up the quilt and trim away all excess batting and backing. Add binding to complete the quilt. See Construction Basics (pg. 102) for binding instructions.

double
churn dash

For the tutorial and everything
you need to make this quilt visit:
www.msqc.co/blocksummer18

Here in Missouri, storms roll in slowly. Dark clouds gather across the fields in ominous clusters, and thunder rumbles and shakes the ground from miles away.

When the kids were young, we loved to sit out on the covered porch to watch the storm. Every time we spotted a flash of lightning, we began to count until we heard the boom of the thunder. "One-Mississippi, two-Mississippi, three-Mississippi . . . " They say every five seconds means the lightning is about one mile away, and we loved to watch the storm move and count the distance.

Then came the rain. At first it was just a drop or two, leaving big wet circles on the dry sidewalk. Soon, however, it fell in heavy, silver sheets that whipped in the wind and sprinkled our faces every now and again.

Then, as suddenly as it came, the storm would wander off across the fields, leaving everything in sight absolutely waterlogged.

Right in front of our house there was quite a dip in the road. A heavy rain would fill that dip right up so it looked like a

harmless little puddle, when in fact it was quite deep. As terrible as it sounds, we loved to sit and watch as unsuspecting cars came zooming through the dip at full speed. The splash was incredible! Water would explode in every direction. "I give that car an 8.5," one of us would say like an Olympic judge. "THAT one was definitely a 10!"

I'll never forget there was a little boy just down the road who used to grab his fishing pole after a heavy rainstorm. With his brows furrowed in concentration, he would lower his line down and wait to catch a fish in the puddle in front of his house. "There are no fish in our puddles, sweetie," his mom would call out the screen door, but he persisted.

One day, after a heavy rainstorm, his older brother snuck a trout from last week's fishing trip out of the freezer. He grabbed a fishing pole, ran out to the puddle, slipped the hook into the fish's mouth, and tossed that icy fish right into the water. When everything was ready, he stood up, took hold of the pole, and called, "Come quick! I think I've got something!"

The little boy came running out of the house, snatched the fishing pole from his brother's hands, and yanked that trout right out of the water. "I knew it!" he cried triumphantly. We thought we'd die trying to hold in our laughter!

From puddles to rainbows to acres of perfectly splashable mud, there's always fun to be had after a storm!

materials

QUILT SIZE
68″ x 88″

BLOCK SIZE
20″ finished

QUILT TOP
1 roll of 2½″ print strips
2¾ yards background fabric
1¼ yards contrasting solid fabric

BORDER
1¼ yard

BINDING
¾ yard

BACKING
5½ yards - vertical seam(s)

SAMPLE QUILT
Bloom Bouquet by Color Pop Studio
for Blank Quilting

1 cut

From the background fabric, cut:

- (3) 10″ strips across the width of the fabric – subcut each strip into 10″ squares. Each strip will yield 4 squares and a **total of 12** are needed.

- (24) 2½″ strips across the width of the fabric

From the contrasting solid fabric, cut:

- (3) 10″ strips across the width of the fabric – subcut each strip into 10″ squares. Each strip will yield 4 squares and a **total of 12** are needed.

- (2) 4½″ strips across the width of the fabric – subcut each strip into 4½″ squares. Each strip will yield 8 squares and a **total of 12** are needed.

2 make strip sets

Sew a 2½″ background strip to a 2½″ print strip along the length. **Make 24.** Press the seam allowance toward the darker fabric. **2A**

2A

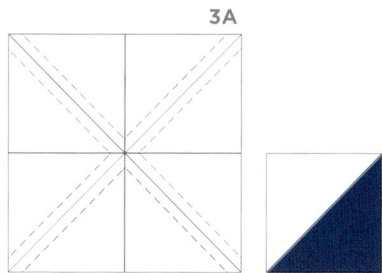
3A

4E

4A

4B

4C

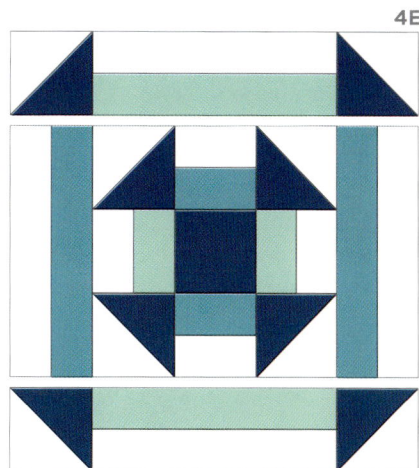
4D

Cut each strip set into the following increments:

- (2) 4½" x 12½" rectangles

- (2) 4½" squares

Stack all matching prints together and set aside the remainder of each strip set for another project.

3 make half-square triangle units

Draw a line from corner to corner twice on the diagonal on the reverse side of the 10" background squares. Layer a marked 10" background square with a 10" solid square with right sides facing. Sew on both sides of each of the drawn lines using a ¼" seam allowance. When finished, cut the sewn square in half vertically and horizontally. Then cut on the drawn lines. Open each to reveal one half-square triangle unit. Press the

seam allowance toward the darker fabric and square up each unit to 4½". Each set of sewn squares will yield 8 half-square triangle units and a **total of 96** are needed for the quilt. 3A

4 block construction

Pick up 2 stacks of matching strip sets. Sew a 4½" half-square triangle unit to either end of 2 matching 4½" strip set squares. 4A

Sew 2 other matching 4½" strip set squares to both sides of a 4½" solid square. 4B

Sew the 3 rows together to complete the center of the block. 4C

Sew a matching 4½" x 12½" rectangle to both sides of the center. Notice the prints match the pieces used at the top and bottom of the center churn dash. 4D

Stitch a 4½" half-square triangle unit to either end of the remaining 4½" x 12½" matching rectangles in your stack. Sew 1 to the top and 1 to the bottom to complete the block. **Make 12.** 4E

Block size: 20" finished

1 Sew a half-square triangle unit to either end of a 4½" strip set. Make 2 that use matching strip sets.

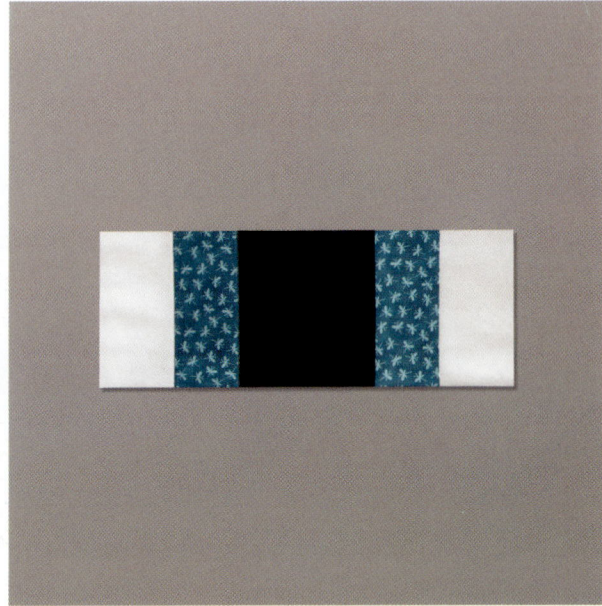

2 Sew 2 other matching strip sets to both sides of a 4½" solid square.

3 Stitch the 3 rows together to complete the center of the block.

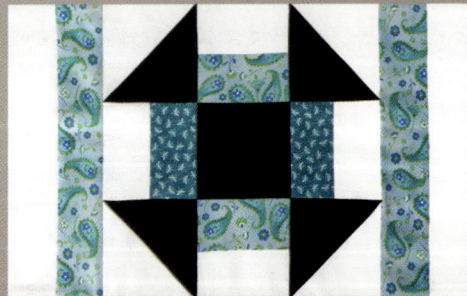

4 Add a matching 4½" x 12½" strip set to both sides of the center unit. Notice the prints match the pieces used at the top and bottom of the center churn dash.

5 Sew a 4½" half-square triangle unit to either end of the remaining 4½" x 12½" matching rectangles in the stack. Sew 1 to the top and 1 to the bottom to complete the block.

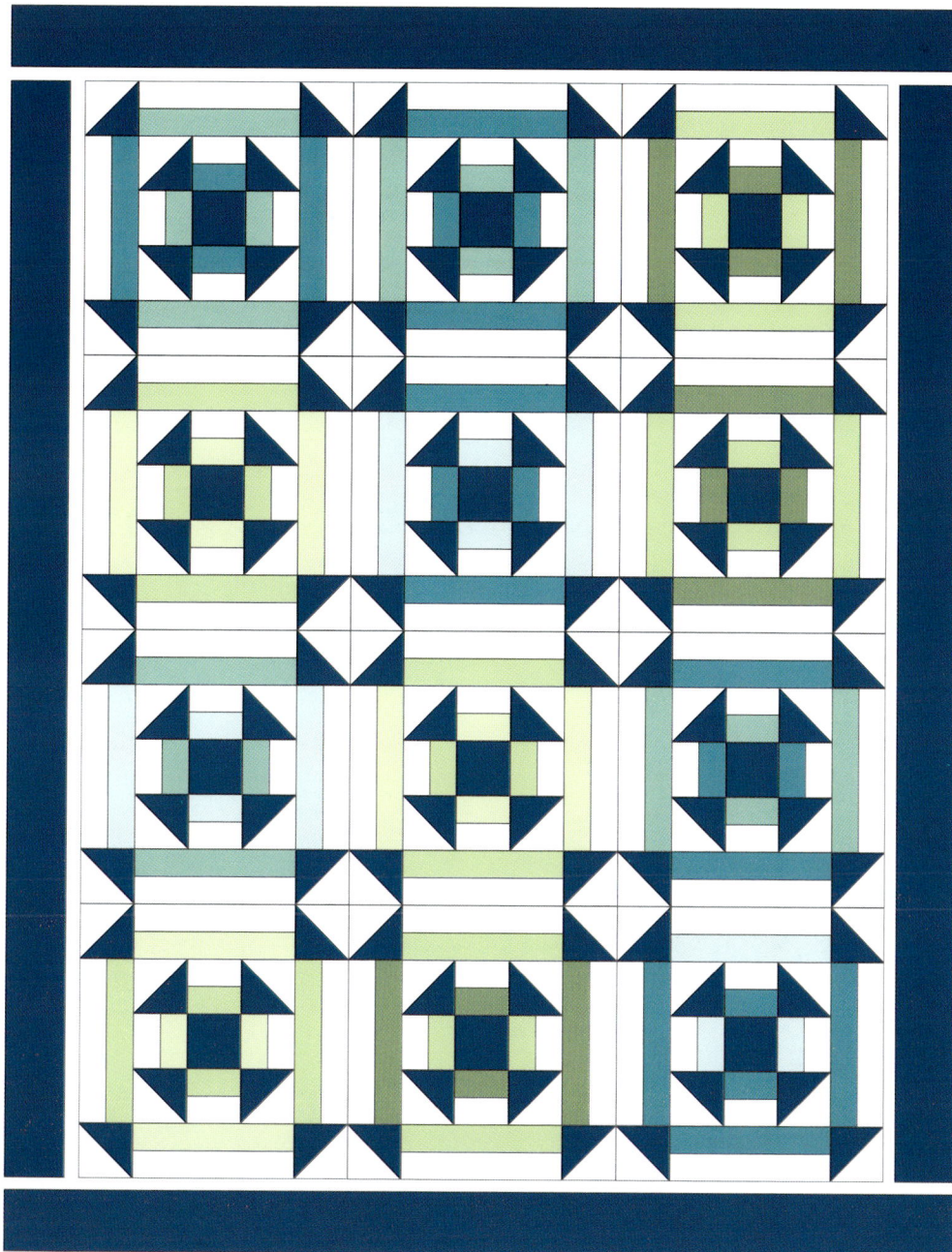

5 arrange and sew

Lay out the blocks in 4 rows with each row made up of 3 blocks. When you are happy with the arrangement, sew the blocks into rows. Press the odd rows toward the right and the even rows toward the left to make the seam allowances "nest." Sew the rows together.

6 border

Cut (8) 4½" strips across the width of the fabric. Sew the strips together end-to-end to make one long strip. Trim the borders from this strip.

Refer to Borders (pg. 102) in the Construction Basics to measure and cut the outer borders. The strips are approximately 80½" for the sides and approximately 68½" for the top and bottom.

7 quilt and bind

Layer the quilt with batting and backing and quilt. After the quilting is complete, square up the quilt and trim away all excess batting and backing. Add binding to complete the quilt. See Construction Basics (pg. 102) for binding instructions.

stars
& stripes

When the time for the State Fair rolls around again in late summer, I find myself singing the words to the Rodgers and Hammerstein musical of the same name, "Our state fair is a great state fair! Don't miss it, don't even be late." I've become a bonafide country girl at heart and I love going to see all the animals, exhibits, and attractions, but most of all, I love that first bite into a delicious funnel cake!

State fairs have been around for more than a century, reminding us of our agricultural heritage and taking us back to our roots. Seeing the rows and rows of beautifully baked pies and colorful preserves in jars makes me smile. I am so glad that people still care enough to make their own handcrafted jams and jellies. It gives me hope for our busy, preoccupied society. To take the time and effort to create something homemade is always worth it. Back in the day, I often entered my Home Economics projects in sewing and cooking in the fair and I even won a few ribbons. It was a great confidence builder and helped me learn more about hard work and improving my skills.

For the tutorial and everything you need to make this quilt visit:
www.msqc.co/blocksummer18

I always take my time admiring the painstakingly hand-stitched quilts on display at the fair. Some have been made for the fair that very year and some are antique quilts, saved through the generations to take their place among all the others. I find the mix of old and new so inspiring. Just because a quilt was made in a certain way 100 years ago, doesn't mean that we have to do it the same way now, but it also doesn't mean that we should avoid hand stitching altogether. There's a time and a place for everything and the fair reminds me of that very idea.

The animals are also a big part of the state fair for me. Seeing all the fluffy, little bunnies in their cages with cute name tags gives me a glow of pride for the youth in 4-H who care so well for them. It's apparent to me that these kids are learning so much and becoming wonderful leaders in their community. My friend Becky has a son who raises champion show pigs for 4-H and it's amazing to see this young man's confidence when he shows one of his prized hogs.

When it's all said and done, there's nothing better than settling into the grandstands with a corndog and watching the rodeo as the sun goes down. The whole experience really makes me appreciate where I live and the rich traditions of this amazing state.

materials

QUILT SIZE
55" x 67"

BLOCK SIZE
11" finished

QUILT TOP
1 roll of 2½" print strips
1 yard background fabric
or ¾ yard background fabric
and (1) 84 ct. package of 2½"
background Mini Charms by
Robert Kaufman

BINDING
¾ yard

BACKING
3½ yards – horizontal seam(s)

SAMPLE QUILT
Enchanted by Kanvas Studio
for Benartex Fabrics

1 cut

From the background fabric, cut:

- (4) 4" strips across the width
  of the fabric – subcut each strip
  into 4" squares. Each strip will
  yield 10 squares and a **total of
  40** are needed

If you bought 2½" mini charms of
background fabric, skip this step.

(5) 2½" strips across the width of the
fabric – subcut each strip into 2½"
squares. Each strip will yield 16 squares
and a **total of 80** are needed

Set aside the remaining fabric for the
border.

From the print strips, select 10 dark
strips from the roll. From each dark
strip, cut:

- (4) 2½" x 6" rectangles
- (4) 2½" x 4" rectangles

Keep all matching prints stacked
together.

2 block construction

For each star block, fold (8) 2½"
squares once on the diagonal. Press the
crease in place to mark the sewing line.
2A

Select a stack of rectangles. Place a
2½" creased background square on 1
end of a 2½" x 6" rectangle with right

2A

2B

2C

2D

2E

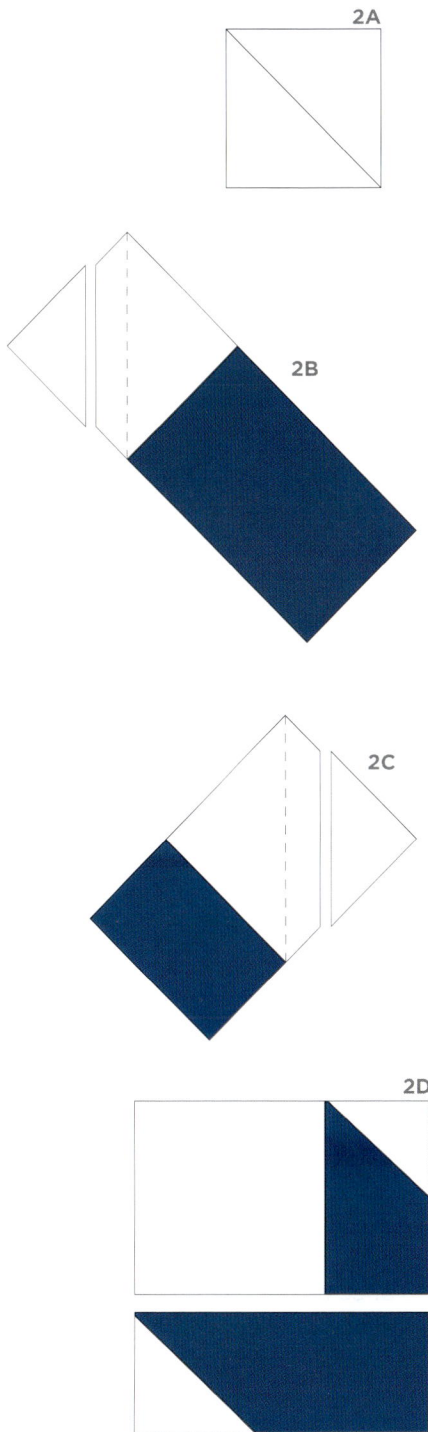

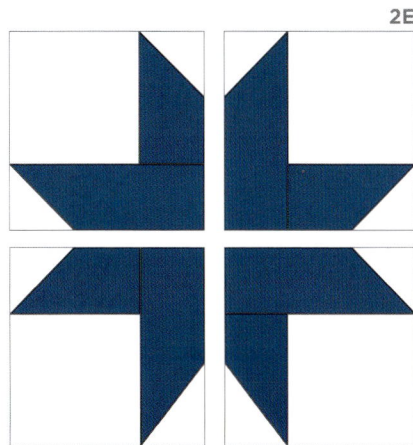

sides facing as shown. (Notice the angle the square is sewn onto the rectangle.) Sew on the crease, then trim ¼" away from the sewn seam. Open and press the seam allowance toward the print. **Make 4. 2B**

Place a 2½" square on 1 end of the 2½"x 4" rectangles with right sides facing as shown. (Notice the angle of the square is opposite of that you stitched onto the 6" rectangles.) Sew on the crease, then trim ¼" away from the sewn seam. Open and press the seam allowance toward the print. **Make 4. 2C**

Sew a short rectangle to a 4" background square. Add a long rectangle as shown. This makes up one quadrant of the block. **Make 4. 2D**

Sew the 4 quadrants together to complete the block. **Make 10** and set aside for the moment. **2E**

Block Size: 11" finished

3 strip set section

Select 14 light strips and 14 medium to dark strips from the roll. Sew the strips together along the length, alternating the lights and the medium to dark strips. After the 28 strips have been sewn together, square up the ends, trimming all selvages away in the process.

🐤 **NOTE:** *The strip set should be approximately 42½" wide after squaring up. If not, you may have to adjust the width of the sashing strip.*

From the remaining background fabric, cut:

- (2) 2½" strips across the width of the fabric. Sew the 2 pieces together to make a sashing strip

Measure the strip set section from top to bottom. It should be approximately 56½". From the 2½" sashing strip, cut a piece to match your measurement and sew it to the left of the section. Refer to the diagram on page 63. There will be some of the strip left over. Set it aside for the moment.

4 putting it all together

Sew 5 star blocks together into a horizontal row. Make 2 rows. See the diagram on page 63, if necessary.

61

1   Mark a 2½" background square from corner to corner once on the diagonal on the reverse side. Place the marked square atop a 2½" x 6" rectangle with right sides facing. Sew on the line, trim the excess away ¼" from the sewn seam.

2   Place a marked 2½" square atop a 2½" x 4" rectangle with right sides facing. Sew on the line, then trim as before.

3   Sew a short rectangle unit to a 4" background square. Add the long rectangle to the bottom as shown. This makes up 1 quadrant of the block. Make 4.

4   Sew the 4 quadrants together as shown to complete one star.

5   Select 14 light strips and 14 medium strips sew them together along the length. Alternate the color values as you sew.

Pick up the remaining piece of the 2½" sashing strip and trim off a piece that measures 2½" x 11½". Stitch the piece to the end of one of the star rows. Sew that row to the left of the strip set section vertically, making sure the plain rectangle is on the bottom. If necessary, trim the plain rectangle so the row of stars fits perfectly with the sewn strips. See the diagram to your left.

Add the remaining row of stars to the top of the quilt.

5 quilt and bind

Layer the quilt with batting and backing and quilt. After the quilting is complete, square up the quilt and trim away all excess batting and backing. Add binding to complete the quilt. See Construction Basics (pg. 102) for binding instructions.

For the tutorial and everything you need to make this quilt visit: www.msqc.co/blocksummer18

summer
school

There's a popular song I've heard that goes something like, "Don't go chasing waterfalls," but the truth is, I would love to do that very thing! I've seen some spectacular sights in my life, but standing before a majestic waterfall and feeling the cool spray on my face has got to be one of my favorite things. It's just breathtaking. The roar of the water blocks out almost every other sound and it's incredibly peaceful.

The tallest waterfall in the world, Angel Falls, is in far-off Venezuela. At 3,212 feet high, it's taller than the Burj Khalifa in Dubai, the tallest building in the world! That's simply amazing to me. Although I've never been there myself, I have seen some spectacular sights a bit closer to home.

Every summer during my teen years, our family would rent a cabin in Lake Tahoe and spend a week there. As the second deepest lake in the United States, it's truly an impressive place. It's so large that in some places it's actually hard to see the opposite shoreline. The water is deep turquoise and it's as pure and clean as most bottled water. You could practically scoop up a handful and take a sip!

Going to Lake Tahoe was a really magical time for me. That lake is so clear and the swimming is amazing. Our cabin was up a trail on the side of a hill and I remember we would run down that dusty trail right into the water. It wasn't quite as fun going back up, but we would tirelessly run the trail back and forth for what seemed like hours, splashing and playing in the sunshine.

We also made plenty of friends there at the lake because often the same families would come up to visit each summer, so some of them we got to see several years in a row. Going to Lake Tahoe with my family will always be a fond memory.

From towering waterfalls to tiny ponds, I love being near the water. Since I was a child, I've taken to the water like a little fish (Fish is my maiden name, after all!) and that love of swimming has stayed with me throughout the years. You won't find me shying away from the edge of the pool when kids start splashing; I'll jump right in with them! This summer, even if it's just a little kiddie pool, go ahead, dip your toes in and don't be afraid to splash around a little!

materials

QUILT SIZE
42½" x 48¼"

BLOCK SIZE
5¾" finished

QUILT TOP
1 package 5" print squares
1¾ yards background fabric

BORDER
¾ yard

BINDING
½ yard

BACKING
2¾ yards - horizontal seam(s)

SAMPLE QUILT
Sunnyside Ave. by Amy Smart for
Penny Rose Designs

1 cut

From each of the 5" print squares cut:

- (4) 2½" squares – trim 2 of the
  squares down to 1¾". Keep all pieces
  cut from the same print square
  stacked together.

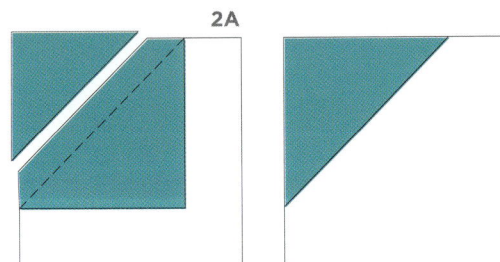

From the background fabric, cut:

- (8) 2½" strips across the width of
  the fabric – subcut each strip into 2½"
  squares. Each strip will yield 16
  squares and a **total of 126** are
  needed.

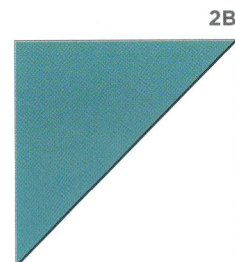

2A

2B

2C

2D

2E

2F

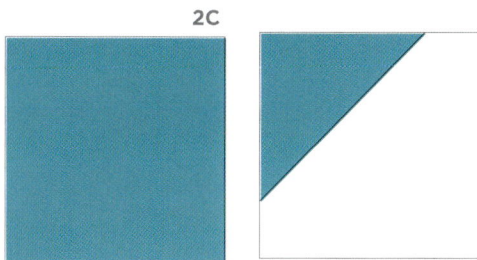

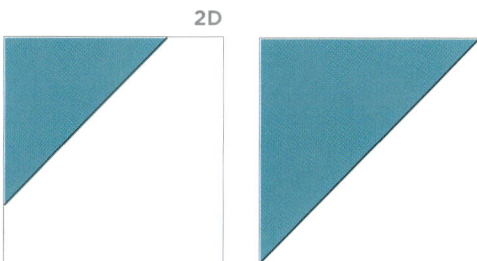

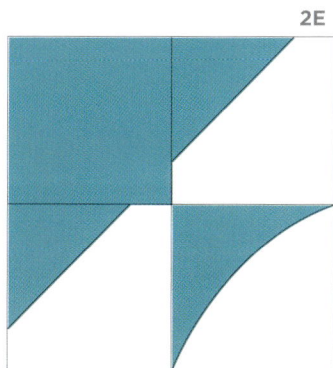

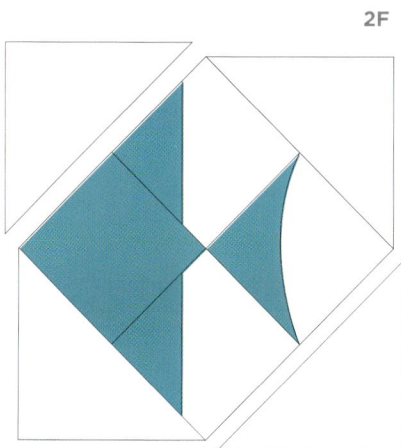

- (9) 4″ strips across the width of the fabric – subcut each strip into 4″ squares. Each strip will yield 10 squares and a **total of 84** are needed.

2 block construction

Pick up a stack of cut print pieces and (3) 2½″ background squares. Fold the 2 smaller print squares once on the diagonal and press the crease in place. The crease line will be your sewing line.

Place a creased print square atop a 2½″ background square with right sides facing. Sew on the crease, then trim the excess fabric away ¼″ from the sewn seam. Open and press. Make 2 fin units. **2A**

Make a tail unit by folding a print 2½″ square in half once on the diagonal with wrong sides facing. Pin the folded square to a 2½″ background square. **2B**

Sew a fin unit to a 2½″ print square. Press the seam allowance toward the print square. **2C**

Sew a fin unit to the tail unit. Press the seam toward the tail. Sew the 2 units together as shown. **2D**

Roll back the folded edge of the print square on the tail unit and top stitch along the curve to complete 1 fish. **2E**

Pick up (2) 4″ background squares. Cut each square once on the diagonal to make setting triangles. Sew a setting triangle to 2 sides of the fish. Sew the remaining 2 triangles to the other 2 sides of the fish. Complete the block by squaring it to 6¼″.
Make 42. 2F

3 arrange and sew

Lay out the blocks in rows with each row made up of 6 blocks. Make 7 rows. Press the seam allowances of the odd rows toward the left and the even rows toward the right to make the seams nest. Sew the rows together.

4 border

Cut (5) 4½″ strips across the width of the fabric. Sew the strips together end-to-end to make one long strip. Trim the borders from this strip.

Refer to Borders (pg. 102) in the Construction Basics to measure and cut the outer borders. The strips are

1 To make a fin unit, place a marked 1¾" print square atop a 2½" background square. Sew on the marked line then trim away the excess fabric ¼" from the sewn seam.

2 Make a tail unit by folding a print 2½" square in half once on the diagonal. Pin to the corner of a 2½" background square.

3 Sew a fin unit to a 2½" print square. Sew the tail unit to a fin unit.

4 Sew the 2 units together as shown. Roll back the folded edge of the tail and top stitch along the curve to complete the fish.

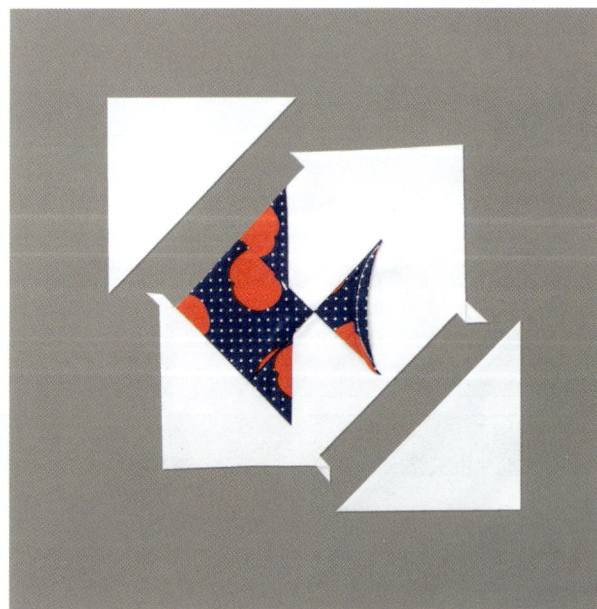

5 Sew a setting triangle to 2 opposing sides of the fish, then add the 2 remaining setting triangle to the other 2 sides. Square each block to 6¼".

approximately 40¾" for the sides and approximately 43" for the top and bottom.

5 quilt and bind

Layer the quilt with batting and backing and quilt. After the quilting is complete, square up the quilt and trim away all excess batting and backing. Add binding to complete the quilt. See Construction Basics (pg. 102) for binding instructions.

charm quilt
on point

I have always had a deep admiration for painstakingly hand-stitched Grandmother's Flower Garden quilts. The hexagon patchwork reminds me of my favorite little creatures, honey bees. To me, they represent the epitome of usefulness while making the world more beautiful at the same time. The work they do is simply miraculous!

I didn't always appreciate bees like I do now. My dad kept bees in our yard and when I was a little girl, I remember being terribly frightened of them. I had never been stung by a bee, but I shied away from them whenever I heard them buzzing around.

One day, I was sitting alongside my dad as he tended the garden, when a bee landed on him. I let out a cry, worried that it would hurt him, but he calmed me down and showed me how docile honey bees can be. He calmly let it crawl all over his hand and then in a quick moment, it flew away. He explained that a bee won't sting unless it's in danger because once it stings, it dies. That profound lesson never left me. It made me realize how precious these creatures are.

For the tutorial and everything you need to make this quilt visit:
www.msqc.co/blocksummer18

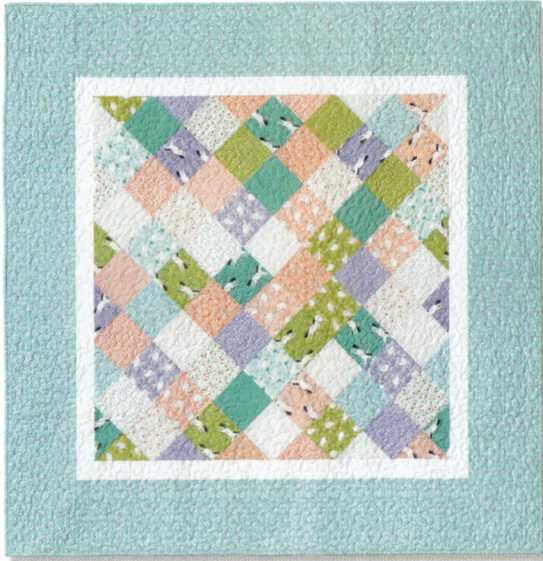

These incredible insects have been around for millions of years. They're as old as the dinosaurs and yet they keep on doing what they do best: pollinating flowers and making honey, to the benefit of us all. Honey is actually the only food made by insects that humans eat, and it's also very nutritionally complex, containing carbohydrates, small amounts of protein, enzymes, vitamins, and minerals.

I love the sweet, rich taste of honey. We've always bought local honey from our neighbors, but I had no idea how much work goes into just one jar. I recently learned that one little worker bee only makes about 1/12 of a teaspoon of honey in her whole lifetime! And an entire hive has to fly about 90,000 miles, the equivalent of three times around the earth, to make just two pounds of honey. Makes me think twice when I put a spoonful in my tea!

Although each bee contributes only a small part of the whole, without all those tiny bees collecting nectar from flowers, no honey would ever be made. So, whenever you feel tempted to think your efforts are insignificant, remember this and realize that we can all do our part to make this world a little sweeter, and your efforts really do matter.

materials

QUILT SIZE
57¾" x 57¾" finished

QUILT TOP
2 packages 5" print squares

INNER BORDER
½ yard

OUTER BORDER
1¼ yards

BINDING
¾ yard

BACKING
3¾ yards - vertical seam(s)

SAMPLE QUILT
Enchanted by Gingiber for Moda Fabrics

1 sew

Sew the 5" print squares into rows. Each row is made up of 6 blocks and 12 rows are needed. While stitching the blocks together, mix up the color values so the lights, mediums, and darks are spread out rather than all grouped together. **1A**

Press the even rows toward the left and the odd rows toward the
right so the seams will "nest." Sew
the rows together to make one large rectangle.

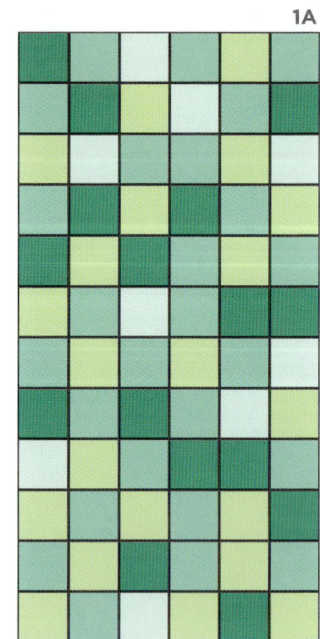

1A

2A

2 mark and cut

Align a ruler with the upper right corner and the lower left corner of the bottom of the 6th row of squares. Make sure the ruler is intersecting the corner of each block. Cut on the diagonal, being careful not to stretch or tug on the edges. See diagram 2A

Without moving the project, realign the ruler with the top of the first square on the left side of row 7 and the bottom of the last square on the right in row 12. Again, make sure the ruler is intersecting the corner of each block. Carefully cut on the diagonal.

Number each section and draw an arrow beside the number so you can keep track of which direction each section is oriented. Refer to the diagram and notice how the sections are numbered. 2B

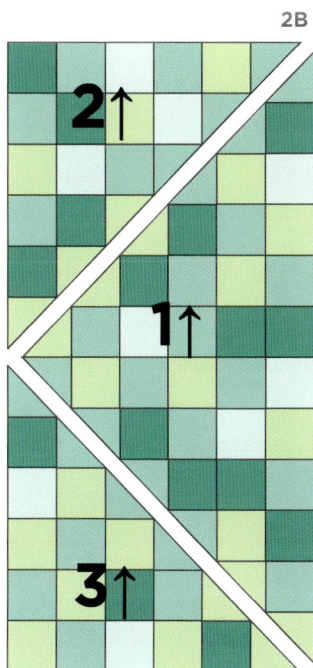
2B

3 rearrange and sew

Pick up Section 3 and place it to the right of Section 1. Make sure the arrows still point in the same direction as before. Pick up Section 2 and place it under Section 3. Refer to diagram 3A

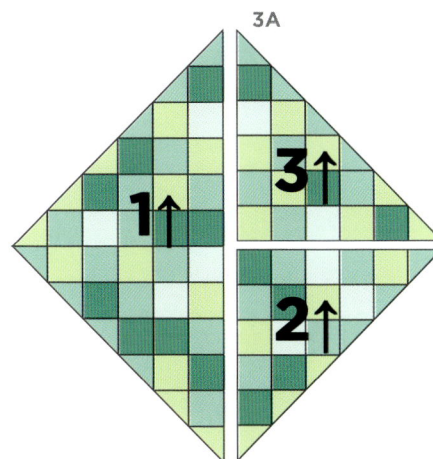
3A

Sew Section 3 and Section 2 together horizontally. Press the seam allowances toward Section 2.

Add Section 1 to the left and sew in place after making sure all block seam allowances are aligned.

4 inner border

Cut (5) 2½" strips across the width of the fabric. Sew the strips together end-to-end to make one long strip. Trim the borders from this strip.

Refer to Borders (pg. 102) in the Construction Basics to measure and cut the inner borders. The strips are approximately 39¼" for the sides and approximately 43¼" for the top and bottom

1 Sew 5″ squares together into rows. Each row is made up of 6 squares and 12 rows are needed.

2 Align a ruler with the upper right corner and the lower left corner of the bottom of the 6th row of squares. Make sure the ruler is going straight through the corners and cut. Realign the ruler with the top of the first square on the left side of row 7 and the bottom of the last square on the right in row 12. Cut.

3 Number each section and place an arrow pointing up alongside the number. Section 2 is the top left, Section 3 is the bottom left and Section 1 is the large center triangle.

4 Rearrange the sections according to number and sew them all back together. Turn the piece 90° and add borders.

5 outer border

Cut (5) 8" strips across the width of the fabric. Sew the strips together end-to-end to make one long strip. Trim the borders from this strip.

Refer to Borders (pg. 102) in the Construction Basics to measure and cut the outer borders. The strips are approximately 43¼" for the sides and approximately 58¼" for the top and bottom.

6 quilt and bind

Layer the quilt with batting and backing and quilt. After the quilting is complete, square up the quilt and trim away all excess batting and backing. Add binding to complete the quilt. See Construction Basics (pg. 102) for binding instructions.

strings
attached

I'd love to say that every Doan family vacation was a blissful time filled with happy faces, scenic byways, and endless sing-alongs, but the truth is, traveling with the entire brood wasn't always a picnic. There were frequent stops along the side of the road for little "emergencies" and detours marked with the familiar refrain, "Are we there yet?"

With our entire bunch in the car, things were always crowded and we were a noisy and rambunctious group, except for my daughter Natalie. She was different from the rest—a bit quieter and definitely more reserved. You'd most likely find her reading a book in whatever corner of the car she happened to be tucked into, or staring serenely out the window at the passing fields and towns, paying no mind to the antics of the rest of the kids.

For the tutorial and everything
you need to make this quilt visit:
www.msqc.co/blocksummer18

On one of our routine stops, we rolled into a gas station in the middle of nowhere for a fill-up, a potty break, and a snack break too. In the midst of the hubbub, Natalie had quietly slipped off to go to the bathroom and freshen up a bit. We didn't notice her missing until we were almost out of the parking lot.

Thankfully, I happened to look back in the rearview mirror just in time to see sweet, quiet Natalie, red-cheeked and running toward the car! She was yelling for us to stop, waving her hairbrush in the air like a traffic controller at

the airport! I let Ron know and he slammed on the breaks before we reached the road. Everyone was surprised to see our little straggler jump back into the car in such a tizzy. Poor thing!

Of course, we wouldn't have gotten far without dear Natalie, but I'll never forget her face in the rearview mirror. It's every parent's nightmare to leave their child behind on accident! The rest of the trip continued without another missing child, and although the car was filled with squirmy, restless children, I was sure glad they were all there with me.

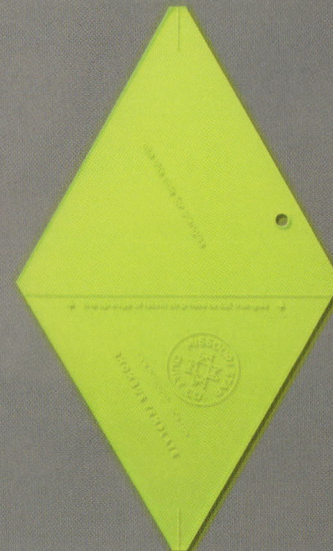

materials

QUILT SIZE
54" x 60"

BLOCK SIZE
4½" x 7¾" finished

QUILT TOP
1¾ yards dark solid
2 yards light solid

BINDING
¾ yard

BACKING
3½ yards - horizontal seam(s)

OTHER
MSQC 10" Rhombus Template

SAMPLE QUILT
Evening Sky, Fern Dark Blue by
Island Batik

1 cut

From the dark solid fabric, cut:

(10) 5" strips across the width of the fabric. Using the rhombus template, cut 6 shapes from each strip for a **total of 60.**

(7) 1½" strips across the width of the fabric. Set aside for sashing strips.

From the light solid fabric, cut:

(10) 5" strips across the width of the fabric. Using the rhombus template, cut 6 shapes from each strip for a **total of 60.**

(9) 1½" strips across the width of the fabric. Set aside for sashing strips.

2 sew

Stitch together a vertical row containing 12 rhombus shapes. Begin with a light shape and alternate with a dark shape. Continue on in this manner until you sew the last shape in place. It should be a dark color. Pay particular attention to the direction the rhombus shapes are placed. We'll call these Row A for clarity. **Make 5 rows. 2A**

2A **2B**

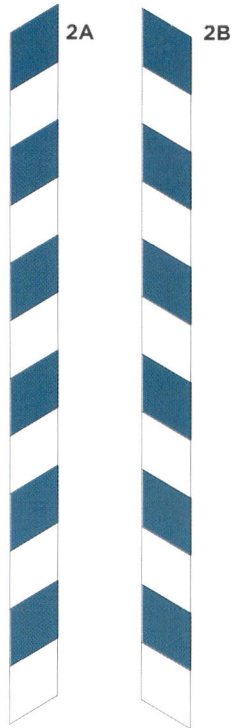

Stitch together a vertical row containing 12 rhombus shapes. Again, begin the row with a light shape and alternate with a dark shape but turn the pieces so they will be mirror images of the pieces in the first rows you made. We'll call these Row B for clarity. **Make 5 rows. 2B**

3 making sashing strips

Sew the 7 dark 1½" strips together into one long strip. Measure the length of each vertical row and cut 4 sashing strips to your measurement. The strips will be approximately 62½" – 64" long.

4A

Sew the 9 light 1½" strips together into one long strip. Measure the length of each vertical row and cut 5 sashing strips to your measurement. The strips will be approximately 62½" – 64" long.

4 lay out and sew

Lay out the quilt top by beginning on the left side with Row A. Follow with a light sashing strip, then add a Row B. Add a dark sashing strip, then add another Row A, followed by a light sashing strip. Continue on in this manner, alternating the A and B rows as well as the color of the sashing strips. Refer to the diagram on page 87, if necessary. Trim the top and bottom of the quilt top evenly with the point of the rhombus shapes that touch the sashing strips. **4A**

5 quilt and bind

Layer the quilt with batting and backing and quilt. After the quilting is complete, square up the quilt and trim away all excess batting and backing. Add binding to complete the quilt. See Construction Basics (pg. 102) for binding instructions.

1   To make Row A, sew 12 rhombus shapes together into a vertical row, alternating the colors. Pay particular attention to the direction the shapes are placed.

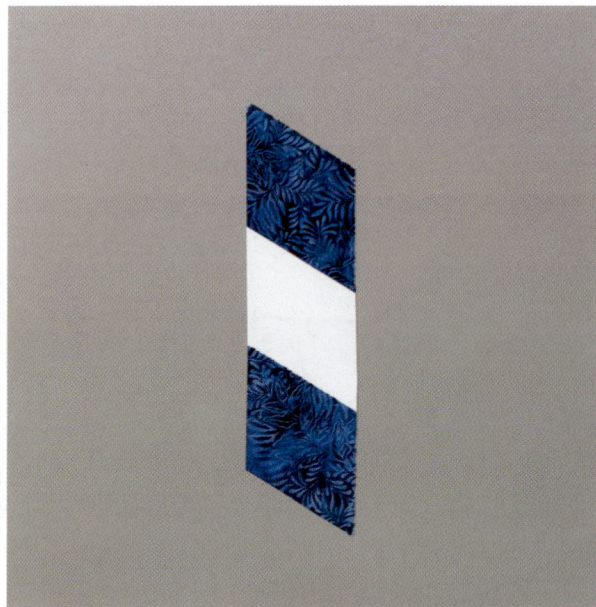

2   Sew 12 rhombus shapes together into a vertical row, alternating the colors. Notice Row B is a mirror image of Row A.

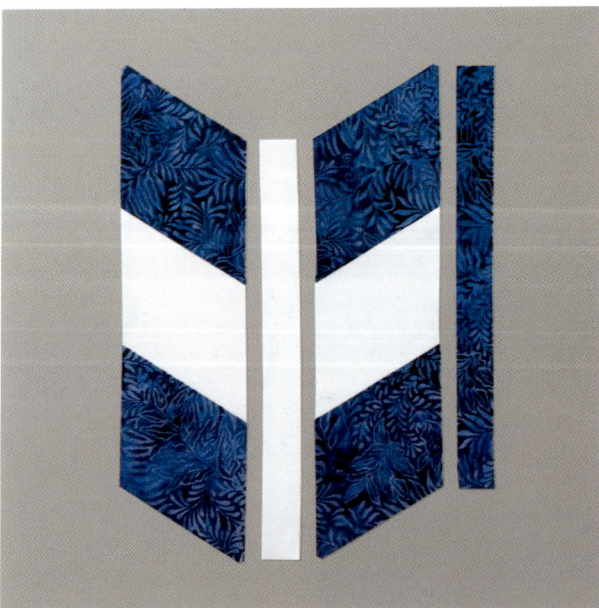

3   After the vertical rows have been made, sew a background 1½" sashing strip between Row A and Row B. Then add a dark sashing strip. Continue in this manner until all sashing strips and rows have been laid out and sewn together.

4   Trim the top and the bottom of the quilt evenly with the point of the rhombus shapes that touch the sashing strips.

sewing hacks

Do you ever have one of those days, sitting at your sewing machine, ripping seams, feeling like nothing is going quite as you planned? Believe me, we all feel this way from time to time! Even though we can't prevent every tough moment, a little planning and ingenuity can go a long way to curing the quilting blues. Over the years, I've gathered a few sewing tips and tricks to help make projects come together in a snap. They've saved me from tears more than once and I have a feeling they'll do the same for you.

Hairspray your thread
Threading a needle is no easy task nowadays when I forget my readers. It seems like a funny thing to do, but a little spritz of hairspray on the end of the thread keeps the tip straight for no-fuss threading.

Stick needles in soap
Are stubborn straight pins giving you a rough time? Run them through a bar of soap and they'll glide through fabric smoothly.

Keep your blades sharp
A project can go from fun to frustrating when your rotary cutter gets dull. I try to keep replacement blades on hand, but when I'm stuck with a dull blade I simply cut through several layers of aluminum foil and voila! It sharpens your blade long enough to buy you a little extra time between replacements, and it works for scissors too!

Organize your bobbins
Heaven knows I have more bobbins than I know what to do with! Keeping them from rolling around and unraveling can help you save your sanity. There are some really smart products for wrangling loose bobbins, but an ice cube tray also works in a pinch!

Pick up pins easily
I know I tend to drop pins as I sew, and picking them up isn't as easy as it used to be. Attach a strong magnet to the end of a yardstick to attract loose pins and you won't find them in the carpet later by accident!

Make a seam allowance guide
Decide where you'd like your seam allowance to be on your sewing machine and stretch a couple large rubber bands around the bed to keep your seams straight. Works with painter's tape too!

Avoid loose spools
Use a ceramic mug or mason jar to hold a larger spool when it won't fit on your sewing machine. It keeps it from rolling off the table and getting tangled.

Make a sewing machine pad
Protect your table and keep your machine running smoothly with an easy-to-make sewing machine pad. It even stores supplies right where you need them for quick access.

sewing machine mat

Size: 20" x 22½"

Note: You will need to measure the base of your sewing machine and adjust the width of the mat as necessary.

SUPPLY LIST
1 yard each of 2 contrasting prints

BINDING
¼ yard

(1) 24" x 34" piece lightweight batting

1 cut

From each yard of the 2 contrasting prints, cut:
• (1) 24" x 32" rectangle

2 layer and sew

Layer the 2 prints and the piece of batting together. Place the piece that is going to be on the back of the mat with the right side facing down, add the batting, then place the piece being used on top with the right side facing up.

Pin the layers together and quilt, using any design of your choice. We stitched lines straight across vertically about 1½" - 2" apart.

After the quilting has been completed, trim away all excess batting and square up the pad so it measures 20" x 30".

3 make binding

Cut (3) 2½" strips across the width of the fabric. Refer to page 102 in the Construction Basics and sew the strips together using the plus sign method. Make 1 long strip. Fold the strip in half lengthwise and press.

Trim 1 piece from the strip that measures the width of the machine mat, about 20" if you are using our measurements. Sew the raw edges to the bottom of the back side of the pad using a ¼" seam allowance. Press the binding strip up and fold it over to the inside of the pad and stitch in place. **3A**

3A

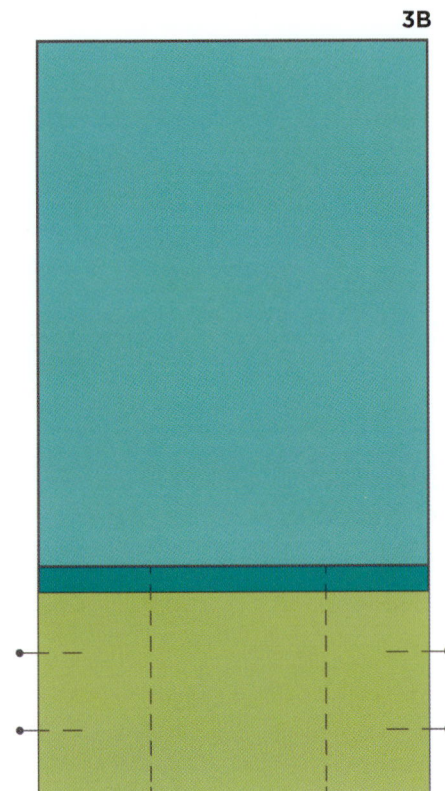

3B

Fold the bottom of the pad up to make a pocket. We made our pocket about 7½" deep. Pin the pocket in place, then stitch along each side. Make compartments in the pocket by stitching from the bottom to the top of the pocket. Make a few backstitches at the beginning as well as the end of each seam line. We made 3 compartments in our pad. The 2 outer compartments are about 6" from the outer edges. This leaves the widest compartment in the center and it measures about 8" wide. **3B**

Add binding to the 3 unfinished sides to complete the mat.

sewing machine foot pedal pocket

Size: 6″ x 6″ finished

SUPPLIES
(2) 6″ squares non-skid shelf liner

BINDING
¼ yard

make binding

Cut (1) 2½″ strip across the width of the fabric. Fold the strip in half lengthwise and press the fold in place. Open the strip. Fold in the raw edge toward the crease and press. Do that for both sides of the strip.

Layer the 2 squares of shelf liner, 1 atop the other. Slip the two pieces into the fold of the binding and pin it in place around 3 sides. Turn and tuck each end of the binding in so the raw edges don't show. Topstitch the binding in place. **1A**

1A

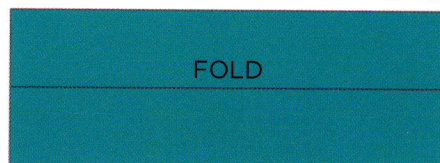

FOLD

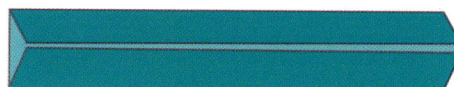

charm quilt on point

QUILT SIZE
57¾" x 57¾" finished

QUILT TOP
2 packages 5" print squares

INNER BORDER
½ yard

OUTER BORDER
1¼ yards

BINDING
¾ yard

BACKING
3¾ yards - vertical seam(s)

SAMPLE QUILT
Enchanted by Gingiber for
Moda Fabrics

QUILTING PATTERN
Cotton Candy

ONLINE TUTORIALS
msqc.co/blocksummer18

PATTERN
pg. 76

double churn dash

QUILT SIZE
68″ x 88″

BLOCK SIZE
20″ finished

QUILT TOP
1 roll of 2½″ print strips
2¾ yards background fabric
1¼ yards contrasting solid fabric

BORDER
1¼ yard

BINDING
¾ yard

BACKING
5½ yards - vertical seam(s)

SAMPLE QUILT
Bloom Bouquet by Color Pop Studio
for Blank Quilting

QUILTING PATTERN
Curly Twirly Flowers

ONLINE TUTORIALS
msqc.co/blocksummer18

PATTERN
pg. 52

easy
breezy
beautiful

QUILT SIZE
76" x 85½"

BLOCK SIZE
9½" finished

QUILT TOP
1 package 10" print squares

INNER BORDER
¾ yard

OUTER BORDER
2 yards

BINDING
1 yard

BACKING
7¼ yards - horizontal seam(s)

OTHER
Scallops, Vines & Waves Template
 by Quilt in a Day
Clover Pen Style Chaco Liner White

SAMPLE QUILT
Club Havana by Patty Young for
Riley Blake Designs

QUILTING PATTERN
Variety B2B

ONLINE TUTORIALS
msqc.co/blocksummer18

PATTERN
pg. 26

HSTs around the world

QUILT SIZE
57" X 69"

BLOCK SIZE
6" finished

QUILT TOP
1 package 10" squares

BORDER
1 yard

BINDING
¾ yard

BACKING
3¾ yards - horizontal seam(s)

SAMPLE QUILT
Blossom Batiks, Splash by Flaurie & Finch for RJR Fabrics

QUILTING PATTERN
Paisley Feather

ONLINE TUTORIALS
msqc.co/blocksummer18

PATTERN
pg. 34

sidekick

QUILT SIZE
59" x 71"

BLOCK SIZE
12" finished

QUILT TOP
3 packages 5" print squares
2 packages 5" background squares

INNER BORDER
½ yard

OUTER BORDER
1 yard

BINDING
¾ yard

BACKING
3¾ yards - horizontal seam(s)

SAMPLE QUILT
High Adventure 2 by Design
by Dani for RIley Blake Designs

QUILTING PATTERN
Pine Tree Meander

ONLINE TUTORIALS
msqc.co/blocksummer18

PATTERN
pg. 44

spring rain

QUILT SIZE
82" x 94"

BLOCK SIZE
10" finished

QUILT TOP
1 package 10" squares
3 yards background fabric
1¼ yards contrasting print

OUTER BORDER
1½ yards

BINDING
¾ yard

BACKING
7½ yards - horizontal seam(s)
or 2½ yards 108" wide

SAMPLE QUILT
Chantrell by Anne Rowan for
Wilmington Prints

QUILTING PATTERN
Meandering Leaves

ONLINE TUTORIALS
msqc.co/blocksummer18

PATTERN
pg. 18

stars
& stripes

QUILT SIZE
55" x 67"

BLOCK SIZE
11" finished

QUILT TOP
1 roll of 2½" print strips
1 yard background fabric
or ¾ yard background fabric
and (1) 84 ct. package of 2½"
background Mini Charms by
Robert Kaufman

BINDING
¾ yard

BACKING
3½ yards – horizontal seam(s)

SAMPLE QUILT
Enchanted by Kanvas Studio
for Benartex Fabrics

QUILTING PATTERN
Faster Posies E2E

ONLINE TUTORIALS
msqc.co/blocksummer18

PATTERN
pg. 60

strings attached

QUILT SIZE
54" x 60"

BLOCK SIZE
4½" x 7¾" finished

QUILT TOP
1¾ yards dark solid
2 yards light solid

BINDING
¾ yard

BACKING
3½ yards - horizontal seam(s)

OTHER
MSQC 10" Rhombus Template

SAMPLE QUILT
Evening Sky, Fern Dark Blue by
Island Batik

QUILTING PATTERN
Meandering Flowers

ONLINE TUTORIALS
msqc.co/blocksummer18

PATTERN
pg. 84

summer
school

QUILT SIZE
42½" x 48¼"

BLOCK SIZE
5¾" finished

QUILT TOP
1 package 5" print squares
1¾ yards background fabric

BORDER
¾ yard

BINDING
½ yard

BACKING
2¾ yards - horizontal seam(s)

SAMPLE QUILT
Sunnyside Ave. by Amy Smart
for Penny Rose Designs

QUILTING PATTERN
Champagne Bubbles

ONLINE TUTORIALS
msqc.co/blocksummer18

PATTERN
pg. 68

totally tulips

QUILT SIZE
89" X 90"

BLOCK SIZE
9" x 17" finished

QUILT TOP
1 package 10" print squares
¼ yard solid
3½ yards background fabric –
  includes inner border

OUTER BORDER
1½ yards

BINDING
¾ yard

BACKING
2¾ yards - 108" wide

SAMPLE QUILT
Butterfly Dance by Sally Kelly
for Wilmington Prints

QUILTING PATTERN
Paisley Feather

ONLINE TUTORIALS
msqc.co/blocksummer18

PATTERN
pg. 10

construction basics

general quilting

- All seams are ¼" inch unless directions specify differently.
- Cutting instructions are given at the point when cutting is required.
- Precuts are not prewashed; therefore do not prewash other fabrics in the project.
- All strips are cut width of fabric.
- Remove all selvages.

press seams

- Use a steam iron on the cotton setting.
- Press the seam just as it was sewn right sides together. This "sets" the seam.
- With dark fabric on top, lift the dark fabric and press back.
- The seam allowance is pressed toward the dark side. Some patterns may direct otherwise for certain situations.
- Follow pressing arrows in the diagrams when indicated.
- Press toward borders. Pieced borders may demand otherwise.
- Press diagonal seams open on binding to reduce bulk.

borders

- Always measure the quilt top 3 times before cutting borders.
- Start measuring about 4" in from each side and through the center vertically.
- Take the average of those 3 measurements.
- Cut 2 border strips to that size. Piece strips together if needed.
- Attach one to either side of the quilt.

- Position the border fabric on top as you sew. The feed dogs can act like rufflers. Having the border on top will prevent waviness and keep the quilt straight.
- Repeat this process for the top and bottom borders, measuring the width 3 times.
- Include the newly attached side borders in your measurements.
- Press toward the borders.

binding

find a video tutorial at: www.msqc.co/006

- Use 2½" strips for binding.
- Sew strips end-to-end into one long strip with diagonal seams, aka the plus sign method (next). Press seams open.
- Fold in half lengthwise wrong sides together and press.
- The entire length should equal the outside dimension of the quilt plus 15" - 20."

plus sign method

- Lay one strip across the other as if to make a plus sign right sides together.
- Sew from top inside to bottom outside corners crossing the intersections of fabric as you sew. Trim excess to ¼" seam allowance.
- Press seam open.

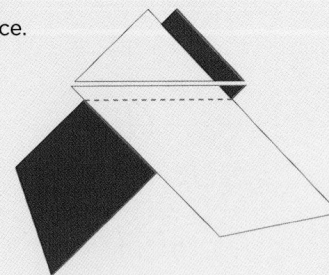

find a video tutorial at: www.msqc.co/001

attach binding

- Match raw edges of folded binding to the quilt top edge.
- Leave a 10" tail at the beginning.
- Use a ¼" seam allowance.
- Start in the middle of a long straight side.

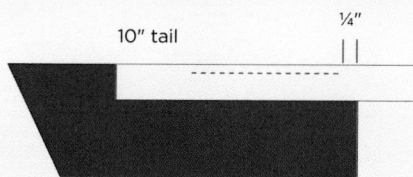

10" tail   ¼"

miter corners

- Stop sewing ¼" before the corner.
- Move the quilt out from under the presser foot.
- Clip the threads.
- Flip the binding up at a 90° angle to the edge just sewn.
- Fold the binding down along the next side to be sewn, aligning raw edges.
- The fold will lie along the edge just completed.
- Begin sewing on the fold.

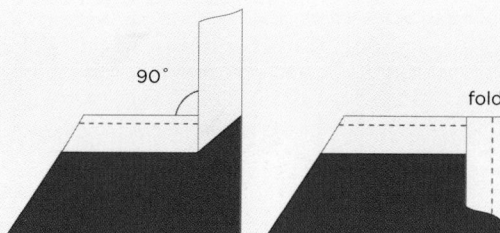

90°   fold

close binding

MSQC recommends The Binding Tool from TQM Products to finish binding perfectly every time.

- Stop sewing when you have 12" left to reach the start.
- Where the binding tails come together, trim excess leaving only 2½" of overlap.
- It helps to pin or clip the quilt together at the two points where the binding starts and stops. This takes the pressure off of the binding tails while you work.
- Use the plus sign method to sew the two binding ends together, except this time when making the plus sign, match the edges. Using a pencil, mark your sewing line because you won't be able to see where the corners intersect. Sew across.

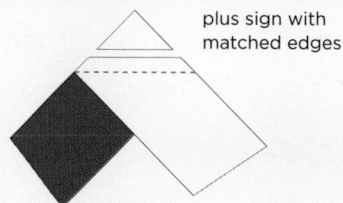

plus sign with
matched edges

- Trim off excess; press seam open.
- Fold in half wrong sides together, and align all raw edges to the quilt top.
- Sew this last binding section to the quilt. Press.
- Turn the folded edge of the binding around to the back of the quilt and tack into place with an invisible stitch or machine stitch if you wish.